God in the New Testament

Neil Richardson

God in the New Testament

EPWORTH PRESS

0 7162 0527 0

First published 1999
by Epworth Press
20 Ivatt Way
Peterborough, PE3 7PG

Typeset by Regent Typesetting, London
Printed and bound in Great Britain by
Biddles Ltd, Guildford and King's Lynn

Contents

Introduction

A book with the title *God in the New Testament* may seem ambitious, to say the least. Mere word-counts are not totally reliable indicators, but the fact that the word 'God' occurs in the New Testament some 1500 times (quite apart from words like 'Lord' and 'Spirit'), gives some indication of the extent of the subject. Nevertheless, the attempt seems worth making, and in this introduction I shall attempt to explain why. In order to do so, it will be useful to set our discussion of the New Testament in the wider context of our situation today in which there is widespread uncertainty, if not incredulity, about God. We shall look at this from three perspectives: first, how we actually use the word *god*, second, why many people today find God incredible, and, third, with reference to our so-called 'post-modern' situation, the reality of God.

1. *Language about God*

The word 'god' is problematic for many people in our culture. Whereas it is obvious to what words like 'table' and 'chair' refer, the referent of the word 'God' is not so obvious. Although the word has acquired certain associations, and is used in certain contexts, it is not self-evident to whom or to what the word *god* refers.

It is helpful to begin by recognizing that the word 'god' is a *generic* word: the kind (*genus*) of 'thing' to which it refers is that which is the object of worship and devotion. Of course, once we begin to insist that there is only one god, or God, the nature of the word changes. In practice it ceases to be a generic word and becomes a name. Both the dimensions of the word 'god' need to be borne in mind. It is worth observing that in the Old Testament Hebrew words for 'god' are basically of two kinds: the word *elohim* (a Hebrew plural) is the generic word, implying, in the first instance, that, of the many gods which existed, one God in particular was the God of Israel. The other word for 'god' was the name *Yahweh* (as it is usually written in Old Testament textbooks), which was replaced eventually in the Greek Old Testament by the word 'Lord'. (See chapter 1 for a brief discussion of this).

In the New Testament the pattern is somewhat different, but the normal word for 'God' is the generic word *theos*, as Paul's reference to 'many gods' in I Corinthians 8.6 shows. The striking feature of the New Testament's language about God, as this book will show, is its expansion and development with reference to Jesus and to the Spirit. For example, the claim of John's Gospel that God has given his 'name' to Jesus, and that he has made it known (John 17.12 and 26), is particularly significant against the Old Testament background.

But to return to our situation, it seems to be stating the obvious to say that belief in one God alone changes everything. Yet it does. At the very least we may observe that if there is only one God, we are likely to be referring not to 'a being', but to Being-itself, as philosophical theology sometimes expresses it. Or, to put this another way, God then is not so much an object amongst other objects (even if by far the most powerful), but in some way an all-encompassing reality in whom everything else lives and moves (compare Acts 17.28).

All this may seem very theoretical and abstract. In fact, it is a very practical issue. Opinion polls continue to show that many people still believe, or profess to believe, in God. It would be misguided and unhelpful to contest that evidence, but it would be simply common-sense to observe that the word 'god' almost certainly means different things to different people. For some, such a belief may be little more than a wistful hope or a nostalgic memory. For others 'God' may function as a protective deity to whom they look in personal crises for help and comfort. For most people in the Western world belief in God is a very private, individual matter. Yet one way of exploring what 'god' actually means to anyone is to examine the practical effect of that 'god' (whoever, or whatever it may be) on their lives. For example, according to the Bible, idols can be identified by their effect on those who worship them. Rather than giving life to their devotees, idols drain it from them. Rather than making them more human, idols make them less than human. (I explore this theme at greater length in chapter 3). More positively, the 'imprint' of *God*, as opposed to idols, on a person's life will be a recurring theme throughout this book.

So, we should not assume that it is self-evident what the word 'god' means, nor what that word means to particular individuals. It is vital to look at the contexts or rather the stories, in which the word *God* is used, and, secondly, to consider the effect that any god has on the lives of those who claim to believe in that god. But now we must look briefly at the second issue before us: the difficulty many people have in believing in God at all.

2. *The credibility of God*

Modern atheism and agnosticism have many roots. Some of the intellectual roots go back a long way. It has recently been argued that theologians of the seventeenth century unwittingly paved the way for modern atheism by attempting to answer philosophical arguments against belief in God by philosophy alone.[1] This does not meant that the church or the Christian should have no truck with philosophy. That would be a short-sighted and narrow view. But Christian faith cannot always (if ever) counter philosophy by philosophy alone. If, however, this theory about theological developments in the seventeenth century is correct, it sheds some light on the long drawn-out arguments of the last three or four centuries about the existence and nature of God.

The Enlightenment tended to cultivate an understanding of human beings as autonomous, rational beings who became increasingly centre-stage ('man the measure of all things'), and the question about *God* tended to become 'Where does God fit in?' After all, there was a powerful tradition, deriving from Aristotle, of God as the 'Unmoved Mover' – i.e. the God who set things in motion, but who was himself unmoved by them. Such a god would always be vulnerable to the riposte of the scientist : 'God? I have no need of that hypothesis'. In any case, if freedom, or autonomy, was increasingly seen as *the* mark of human beings, a 'supernatural' (now a more problematic word) God was bound to be seen as a potential threat to human freedom.

There are other intellectual challenges to belief in God. The influence of Darwin, Freud and Marx has been immense. Even people who have never heard of them let alone read any of their writings are likely to have been influenced by some of their ideas. All three of these men have been widely perceived as developing views of creation, of the human psyche, and of society which are in conflict with received ideas of God. And, of course, there is much truth in this. For example, Darwin's theory of evolution was rightly seen as challenging Genesis 1 as a literal account of how the world was made. The possibility that all three of these important thinkers may have been mistaken in certain respects, or that some of their thought is perfectly compatible with traditional Christian understandings of God has been less widely perceived.

None of this should be taken to imply that all that we need to convince people of the reality of God is better theological arguments (though the urgent need for better theology is all too often ignored). In fact, there are many more reasons why people find it difficult to believe in God today. A busy, noisy, socially-fragmented environment does not help. And if the biblical message about God is true, then living in an affluent society may be expected to create its own spiritual problems. (I am thinking here of New Testament teaching about poverty.) The interaction of outward circumstances and a person's spiritual state, of course, may be complex and subtle, but it is worth noting the comment of a Quaker writer of two generations ago: Thomas Kelly[2] observed that Western people are 'not skilled in the inner life, where the real roots of our problem lie . . . The outer distractions of our interests reflect an inner integration of our own lives. We are trying to be several selves at once, without all our selves being organized by a single, mastering life within us.'

Tragically, of course, the church itself often provides anything but convincing evidence for the existence of God. Its worship is often neither attractive, nor compelling; its preaching is sometimes obscure, irrelevant or simplistic, its fellowship too often unwelcoming and insular, its witness uncertain and unChristlike. The seriousness of this should not be under-estimated. But it is perhaps worth observing that the Christian scriptures offer some very unflattering pictures of 'the people of God', warn that God's reputation or credibility is at stake in the way they conduct themselves in the world, but still testify to what they insist is the revealed reality of God.

In the kind of environment I have all too briefly sketched, it is not easy for Christians or, indeed, any religious people, to find their way. It is important not to paint too bleak a picture. The church, for all its failings, continues to draw people to faith, and human goodness keeps on welling up, often in unlikely places and, for the Christian, that in itself is an intimation of God . Nevertheless, these are not easy days, in the so-called Western world at least, for Christian faith and the church, and there is an urgent need to re-appropriate, at all levels of the church and, indeed, of life, the biblical understanding of God.

But finally in this introductory survey of the context in which we find ourselves, we need to confront the most fundamental question of all, the reality of God.

3. *The reality of God*

Two features, in particular, of our so-called post-modern situation merit our attention. First there has been a sharp reaction in the twentieth century in both theology and philosophy against *metaphysics* and meta-narratives. The very term metaphysics is a matter of dispute, but it may be defined as the study or exploration of what, if anything, there is beyond what can be observed. Philosophy, particularly in the middle years of this century, concentrated on language, dismissing as meaningless what could not be ascertained by empirical observation. Theology tended to concentrate on revelation and experience, often ignoring the fundamental metaphysical question *What is there?* as unnecessary or irrelevant. But if theology is to be truly theology, its legitimate sphere of inquiry is nothing less than reality itself, whatever that might be.

A second feature of our context is the tendency in post-modern thought towards relativism. Thus 'doing your own thing' is applied to religious belief and practice; hence the notion of truth *relative* to the individual ('this is true for me'). So far from the truth being 'out there' (as a popular TV programmme has it), the truth is what you make it. It is perhaps not surprising that, in such a cultural climate, some theologians have suggested that God isn't there at all; rather,

God is simply a symbol representing value, meaning, and so on.

In response to all this, the Christian believer needs firmly to embrace the traditional conviction that Christian faith is concerned with reality and truth. That claim cannot be proved (or disproved), otherwise it would not be faith, and strident, dogmatic assertions need to be replaced by quieter, gentler expressions of what Christians believe to be true and to experience as truth. But in order for that to happen, some hard work needs to be done at both the spiritual and intellectual levels – and the two cannot be easily separated. The shallowness, uncertainty and tentativeness of much of our contemporary experience of God needs urgently to be addressed. And, secondly, we need to recognize how Christian theism – that is, our received understanding of who and what God is – has often been seriously diminished and distorted in modern times.

Many years ago, I was rash enough to invite a group of people to discuss 'What do we mean by God?' Two people present were, perhaps not surprisingly, quite nonplussed by the question. 'We came tonight', they said, 'because we hoped you would tell us.' Of course, 'a god comprehended is no god'. Nevertheless, the Christian will at least want to say that God is the source and sustainer of life, truth, meaning, value and beauty, that the mystery of God is the central mystery of Christian faith, and that God is the key to the life and well-being ('salvation') of the world. The revelation of God is the central theme of the New Testament, and to its writings we now turn.

I

Jesus and his God

The New Testament has more to say about God than about any other subject except Jesus. So it is surprising that relatively little has been written on the subject, compared, say, with the vast outpourings on the historical Jesus, Paul and the Law, the literary relationship between the first three Gospels (the so-called 'Synoptic Problem'), and other themes which help to keep a New Testament industry going. Of course, theology in the broadest sense comes into most things, particularly our understanding of who Jesus was, and what the New Testament has to say about the way human beings should live. But the New Testament understanding of God has not received the attention it deserves.

My concern is to map out the broad contours of what the New Testament says about God, and to do so in three ways. The first is a linguistic one: to explore the kind of language the New Testament uses about God or, since *theos* (the Greek word for 'god') is so overwhelmingly predominant, to ask in what ways and in what contexts language about God is used. There is a particular reason for adopting this approach. In any religious tradition the word 'God' acquires a certain significance, deriving from the accumulated experience, traditions and rituals of the individuals and people who stand in that tradition. That was true of the Jewish people. A question implicitly raised by the New Testament but rarely addressed today is whether the New Testament's claim of a new revelation of God (and it can hardly be denied that that claim is there) carries with it a new understanding of God. Is the old simply seen in clearer focus? Or is something now seen and known which was not known and seen before? The safest answer which avoids the opposing extremes of conforming the New Testament to the Old, or rejecting the Old Testament altogether, is to say that there is both continuity and discontinuity between the Jewish and Christian understandings of God. But of what precisely does that continuity and discontinuity consist?

My second approach is a kind of 'theology from below'. I assume that whatever a person worships shapes that person's life in certain ways. What a person worships may sometimes be deduced from the imprint of that reality (even if that reality is an idol) upon that person's life. How a person lives may reflect, should reflect, or will reflect, that person's god. In this book I shall be exploring what we may deduce about God from the *imprint* of God on the two principal characters of the New Testament, namely Jesus and Paul.

The third way of studying this question is a synthetic one. I shall be examining not just one New Testament writer, nor studying several in isolation from one another, but attempting to relate what one writer has to say to the message of another.

It seems natural, however, to begin with the teaching of Jesus about God, and that will be our concern in this chapter. The amount of material, of course, is vast, and scholars tend to concentrate on one fragment or one theme. So there may be something to be said for making the foolhardy attempt to offer an overview, even if it is like trying to summarize the plays of Shakespeare.

The language Jesus used about God seems to have been of four kinds. But these four categories, odd though it may seem, do not include the simple expression 'God' (*ho theos*), and it may be useful to outline why this is so.

In the Old Testament, as is clear from most translations,

there are two very common expressions for God: one is the simple word 'God' (the Hebrew for which is *elohim*), and the other the title 'the Lord' (Hebrew *adonay*, literally 'my lord'). But whereas *elohim* was the general word for 'god', 'the Lord' was, in fact, a substitute expression, replacing the proper name of Israel's God, *Yahweh*. The Hebrew text retained the original consonants YHWH, but what was read (and most reading then was aloud) was 'the Lord'. The Greek translation of the Old Testament, made in the third century BC, may have kept the original Hebrew consonants (this is disputed) every time *Yahweh's* name occurs in the text, but there is no doubt that, again, what was read was 'the Lord' (Greek *ho kurios*).

Exodus 3.13–14 is the only passage which attempts to explain the origin and meaning of YHWH:

> Moses said to God, 'If I come to the Israelites and tell them that the God of their forefathers has sent me to them, and they ask me his name, what am I to say to them?' God answered, 'I am that I am. Tell them that I am has sent you to them.'

Jews believed that this name of God was too holy to be spoken: even when the scriptures were being read or quoted, various strategies were employed to enable the reader or speaker to avoid uttering the sacred name. Even the normal Hebrew word for 'God', *elohim*, seems to have been avoided in everyday speech. If this was so, what words or expressions did Jesus use for 'God'?

Many years ago, Gustaf Dalman[1] pointed out that Jews used a variety of circumlocutions for the words 'Yahweh' and 'God' such as 'Heaven' and 'the Name'. (This can be seen, for example, in the best-known section of the Mishnah, the *Aboth*.)[2] Dalman concluded that, where the Gospels attribute the use of *ho theos* to Jesus, this was an accommodation by the evangelists to their Greek readers or audiences.

What Jesus used instead of *elohim* or *yhwh* is an interesting question. Dalman, in effect, offers three suggestions: 'heavenly Father' (a common enough expression in the Judaism of the time), circumlocutions such as 'the Name' or 'heaven', or, thirdly, the omission of the divine name. (For example, where Matt. 26.61 has 'the Temple of God', it is likely that Jesus said 'this Temple', as in Mark 14.58, or simply 'the Temple': cf. Mark 15.29.)

For this reason, then, I shall not be considering those sayings of Jesus where 'God' may have replaced, or been added to, an earlier expression, although the circumlocutions themselves, where they can be discerned or conjectured, are often instructive. The first category of the 'God-language' of Jesus, however, can reasonably be said to be his 'Kingdom' language, and to that I now turn.

Even when we have allowed for the editorial additions of the evangelists, many such sayings have good claim to go back to Jesus himself. Some, notably Luke 7.28, 11.20, Mark 9.1 and 10.14f., and Matt. 11.12 pass one or more of the so-called criteria of authenticity[3] by virtue of their originality and even awkwardness – i.e. they are unlikely to have been created by the early church. Take, for example, Mark 9.1. 'He said to them, "Truly I tell you: there are some of those standing here who will not taste death before they have seen the Kingdom of God come with power"' reads very much like an unfulfilled prophecy on the lips of Jesus. (Matthew and Luke, if they followed Mark, as is generally believed, have an almost identical saying at Matt. 16.28 and Luke 9.27.) Others, such as Mark 10.23–25, are an integral part of stories which have a strong historical claim. Others belong to, or introduce, parables most of which are likely to derive originally from Jesus himself.

But what did the 'Kingdom of God' denote? In what way may its content and use contribute to our exploration of the New Testament question of God?

There has been a growing consensus in recent years that the phrase 'Kingdom of God'/'Kingdom of Heaven' means 'God in his self-revelation'.[4] The Kingdom, therefore, is not primarily a place, or even an event. It is a present and future reality which people may, or may not perceive, encounter, enter and share. So Jesus taught that God's self-revelation is at hand (Mark 1.15, Matt. 4.17); that if 'I by the finger of God cast out demons' (Luke 11.20/Matt. 12.28) then God's self-revelation has come upon you unawares; that it is like leaven, working subversively in the world (Matt. 13.33/Luke 13.20–21) or wheat amongst the tares – the wheat was there before the tares, and it will survive them (Matt. 13.24–30); it is as mysterious, and as inexorable, as the growth of seed in the earth (Mark 4.26–30) and it costs not less than everything, because God's self-revelation is for those who become nobodies, that is, like children (Mark 10.13–16 and parallels) in the eyes of the world but, like a pearl of great price (Matt. 13.45–46), it is worth everything. It is like a grain of mustard seed, insignificant in its beginnings, yet mightier than an empire (Mark 4.30–32 and parallels).

This substitution of the word 'God' for 'Kingdom of God' seems to fit best those sayings in which the Kingdom of God is the subject, either of sayings like Mark 1.15, or of a parable. It does not seem to fit so well those sayings which describe the Kingdom as a reality to enter, or a place to occupy. How is the 'Kingdom of God' to be understood in sayings such as these?

There are two clues which may help us, one in Mark and one in John. In the sequence of sayings recorded in Mark 9.43–47 it is clear that the word 'life' and the phrase 'the Kingdom of God' are used synonymously: to enter into life is to enter into the Kingdom, and vice versa.

'If your hand causes your downfall, cut it off; it is better for you to enter into life maimed . . . (v.43)'

'And if your eye causes your downfall, tear it out; it is better to enter into the Kingdom of God with one eye . . . (v.47)'

In John a similar process can be seen. The expression 'the Kingdom of God' occurs only twice in this Gospel (3.3 and 5). But up to this point, the phrase 'eternal life' has *not* occurred, whereas, from this point, the expression 'Kingdom of God' does not occur again. Given the flow of the dialogue between Jesus and Nicodemus, and what is subsequently said about 'eternal life', it is reasonable to conclude that the evangelist is saying, in effect: for 'Kingdom of God' now read 'eternal life'.

Can the same phrase be paraphrased sometimes as 'God', sometimes as 'life'? According to the Old Testament, God is the secret and source of human life. Many verses in the Psalms, especially, indicate as much:

For with you is the fountain of life;
in your light we see light (Ps. 36.9).

In the New Testament, verses such as John 1.4 ('in him was life, and that life was the light of humankind'), and 14.6 ('I am . . .Life') repeat the biblical message that God in his self-revelation is the source of life – or, in the New Testament, the source of *eternal* life. The important theological point, to which the New Testament bears witness, is that God's revelation is never an experience which can be observed in a detached way. It invites participation.

To summarize this section of the argument, the Kingdom sayings of Jesus divide broadly into two categories:

1. Those in which the Kingdom is the stated or implied subject. I am suggesting that in these sayings 'Kingdom of God' or 'Kingdom of Heaven' may be paraphrased as 'God in his self-revelation'.

2. Those in which the Kingdom is the object, objective or

goal. In these sayings the Kingdom may be paraphrased as 'life' or 'eternal life'.

Sayings in both categories apply to Jesus, on whose life and ministry, his followers came to believe, the Kingdom was imprinted. (I return to this theme later on.)

I turn next to Jesus' sayings about the Father. The 'Fatherhood' of God has been conspicuous by its absence from many major treatments of the teaching of Jesus in recent years. There are at least two reasons for this state of affairs. The first lies in the contemporary ambivalence, due to the feminist movement, towards male imagery applied to God. The second lies in the recent history of New Testament scholarship. Undoubtedly the most influential contribution to the study of Jesus' language about 'the Father' has been that of Joachim Jeremias. In particular, he popularized the idea that *abba*, the Aramaic word for 'father' included three times in the New Testament, was the childish word for 'father', the English equivalent being 'daddy'. Since Jeremias, there have been scholars who have accepted, more or less uncritically, Jeremias' findings. There are also those who have either ignored them, or rejected them. It is clearly important, if we are to get Jesus' language about God in as sharp a focus as possible, to establish as fully as we can the significance of this 'father' language.

First, the Old Testament and later Jewish background. In the Old Testament, the word 'father' is infrequent both in prayer and in wider language about God. In the period between the Old and New Testaments (the 'inter-testamental' period), however, God is addressed more frequently as 'Father' or as 'Father in heaven'. A number of examples can be given from the Apocrypha: Ecclesiasticus, for example, has 'Lord, Father, and Ruler of my life' (23.1; see also v.4 and Wisd. 2.16). Other examples can be found in non-biblical Jewish writings, such as the rabbinic literature and the Pseudepigrapha (writings so-called because many of them, though written in the last three centuries before, and the first three after Christ, bear the names of Abraham, Moses, Isaiah etc., e.g. the Testament of the Twelve Patriarchs).·

But, second, *how* are these expressions used? In particular, do the sources refer to *the* Father in Heaven, to 'our', 'my' Father or what? G. F. Moore contended, and in this he seems to be correct, that the sources speak, not of '*the* Father in heaven' ('which might express God's relation to the universe'), but of 'my' or 'our' Father.[5] This suggests a covenantal background for the concept of God's Fatherhood.

Thirdly, what of the word *abba*? The work of Jeremias has been very influential, but needs to be corrected in at least two respects:

1. James Barr has pointed out the fallacy of arguing for the meaning of a word from its etymological roots. That is, even if *abba* originated in the babbling talk of a small child, that does not mean it *remained* distinctively, still less exclusively, a childish word. The sources show, and Jeremias himself acknowledged this, that adults, as well as children, used *abba* in addressing their human fathers.

2. The word *abba* was probably not unique as a mode of address to, or a way of referring to God. Here Jeremias relies to a large extent on an argument from silence. The most frequently cited example from Jewish sources of the use of *abba* referring to God is the story of Hanan, grandson of Honi, the circle-drawer:

> When the world was in need of rain, the rabbis used to send school children to him, who seized the train of his cloak and said to him, *Abba, Abba*, give us rain! He said to God: Lord of the universe, render a service to those who cannot distinguish between the *Abba* who gives rain and the *Abba* who does not.

The debate has been a complex and technical one. We would be wrong to argue that Jesus' use of the word *abba* was unique, but there is much to be said for the view that his use of *abba* for God, both in reference to God and prayer to God, was characteristic, distinctive, and even unusual. The appearance of *abba* in two of Paul's letters (Rom. 8.15, Gal. 4.6), together with its retention by Mark in the Gethsemane narrative (14.36) suggests that it was remembered by the early church as an especially significant word. (Barr, *contra* Jeremias, argues that *different* Aramaic forms – i.e. not just *abba* – may lie behind the different Gospel expressions which occur, such as the variants at the beginning of the Lord's Prayer (Luke 11.2, Matt. 6.9). It is perhaps worth adding that John's Gospel, however much it may reflect the elaboration and expansion of Jesus' original words, seems to retain the memory that 'Father' was Jesus' special word for God; most of its occurrences in John are in sayings attributed to Jesus.

So we turn to the evidence of the Gospels. The word 'Father' is much more common in Matthew than in Mark or Luke. In fact all of the four certain references to 'Father' in Mark (11.26 is textually doubtful), have parallels in one or both of the other Synoptic Gospels. Of the references to God as Father in Matthew, some at least must be regarded as the work of the evangelist himself. For example, in Mark 3.31–35 we have the story of the visit of Jesus' mother and brothers coming to see him. Mark's version ends like this: 'Whoever does the will of God is my brother and sister and mother' (v.35). Matthew's equivalent can be found in 12.46–50 and ends 'Whoever does the will of my heavenly Father is my brother and sister and mother.' A similar example can be found in Matthew 15. A careful comparison of Matthew 15.1–20 with Mark 7.1–23 shows that a short section of Matthew, vv.12–14, is an addition to Mark's original version. In that additional section we find the following: 'He answered: "Any plant that is not of my heavenly Father's planting will be rooted up"' (v.13).

There are other examples of this kind, where a later evangelist may well have elaborated on the words of Jesus as found in the earlier evangelist. We cannot be certain, of course, but need to reckon with the possibility that at least some occurrences of 'Father' do not go back to Jesus himself.

Nevertheless, there are good grounds for asserting that this mode of reference to God was fundamental and, in a sense, all-pervasive. (There is a parallel here with the writings of Paul, who uses the term 'Father' sparingly, but almost always in weighty contexts.) T. W. Manson, whose detailed work on the teaching of Jesus is still well worth consulting, posed the dilemma as follows:

> Matthew and John suggest, rightly as I think, that the Fatherhood of God is one of the keys to the Gospel: our primary authorities, Mark and Q, again, I think, rightly, show on the part of Jesus a disinclination to speak of the matter at all except during the latest period of the ministry, and then only to a limited circle of hearers.[6]

Manson is probably right about Jesus' apparent reticence (if that is the right word), and that it was usually to disciples that he spoke about God as Father. But he went beyond the evidence in claiming that Jesus' speaking of God as Father was a post-Caesarea Philippi development. Peter's confession at Caesarea Philippi (Mark 8.27ff. and parallels in Matt. and Luke), may have been a watershed in Jesus' ministry, but it does not seem to have changed the way he spoke about God. Manson's own solution to the surprising infrequency of father-language in the synoptic Gospels is to appeal both to the religious experience of Jesus, arguing that 'the Father' was 'the supreme reality' in the life of Jesus and to other people's religious experience: 'this experience we may comprehend in proportion as we ourselves are made partakers in it'.[7]

There is a further point to be added here, and it is this: what Jesus said or implied about 'the Father' cannot be confined to sayings in which he explicitly uses the word 'father'. The *whole* of Jesus' language about God must be considered since, unless we are to make nonsense of the teaching of Jesus, 'the Father' and 'the Kingdom of God/Heaven' were intended to refer to the same reality. Secondly, what Jesus said or implied about himself, and others, as *sons* may also be said to cast a reflective light on the Fatherhood of God. I return to this theme later on.

Given the few references to 'the Father' in the teaching of Jesus which can be said with reasonable probability to be historically authentic, what can be said about its meaning and significance?

The cryptic saying found in Matt. 11.25–27 (and almost verbatim in Luke 10.22), if authentic, is clearly important. After a brief prayer of thanksgiving, in which Jesus twice addresses God as Father, he goes on to say: 'Everything is entrusted to me by my Father; and no one knows the Son but the Father, and no one knows the Father but the Son, and those to whom the Son chooses to reveal him.'

It is possible that the clause 'No one knows the Son but the Father' is a later addition, although there is something to be said for the view that this and the succeeding clause reflect a particular Oriental way of expressing the intimate, mutual understanding between two people.[8] It is also possible that the original saying was more proverbial in form: 'None knows a son except a father . . .' If this is so, the first part of the saying may reflect a social context in which the skills of a trade, or the responsibilities of a business, were handed on from father to son. Or, similarly, it may reflect a commercial world in which sons regularly acted as agents for their fathers (as in the parable of the wicked husbandmen): 'All things have been entrusted to me by my Father.'

The saying goes on to refer to a mystery of reciprocal

knowledge; it is a mystery, or secret, known only to those who participate in the knowing. So the Fatherhood of God is a mystery, revealed to some, but not an obvious fact known to everyone. This distances the speaker, first, from the Greek world in which to declare Zeus as Father was to recognize that he was the origin of all life. But it is not entirely at home in the world of the Old Testament and Judaism either, where one nation had been taught, on the basis of their covenant, to think of God as their Father. Similarly, there is a mystery about sonship: that is not obvious, either, for 'no one knows who a/the son is except the Father'. So there is a double mystery, since it takes two to make a relationship – the mystery of a revealed relationship. Other language in Matthew deepens the mystery; Jesus in the Sermon on the Mount speaks of 'the Father who is in secret' (6.6 and 18).

When we explore the content of this term for God, it seems to occur in particular contexts:

1. It occurs in the prayers of Jesus, and in teaching about prayer (Matt. 6.9, 7.11, 11.26).

2. It occurs in teaching about forgiveness (Mark 11.25–26; Matt. 6.14–15, 18.35; Luke 15.12ff).

3. It occurs in teaching about God's care and mercy (Matt. 5.43–48, 10.29).

4. It occurs in eschatological sayings, that is, sayings about ultimate things (Mark 13.32; Matt. 10.33, 13.43, 16.27, 25.34, 41; 26.29).

To what extent do these sayings, not all of which, admittedly, may go back to Jesus himself, strike a new note in comparison with the Judaism of Jesus' day?

Two passages, in particular, concern us here. The first is Matt. 5.43–8:

'You have heard that they were told, "Love your neighbour and hate your enemy." But what I tell you is this: Love your enemies and pray for your persecutors; only so can you be children of your heavenly Father, who causes the sun to rise on good and bad alike, and sends the rain on the innocent and the wicked. If you love only those who love you, what reward can you expect? Even the tax collectors do as much as that. If you greet only your brothers, what is there extraordinary about that? Even the heathen do as much. There must be no limit to your goodness, as your heavenly Father's goodness knows no bounds.'

First, the context warns us against drawing facile contrasts between the old and the new: 'I came not to abolish, but to complete (or, fulfil)' (5.17b). And certainly there are some close parallels both in the Old Testament and Judaism to the teaching given here. This is true of both commands: 'Love your enemies' and 'Pray for your persecutors'.[9] So we should conclude that similar teaching in the Old Testament anticipates the teaching of Jesus (as the overall picture of Matt. 5 implies).

What of the statements about God which are contained in this passage? It is worth noting what the passage does *not* say. There is no warrant here; that is, it does not say, 'Love your enemies . . . *because* you are all sons . . .' What we call the universal brotherhood, or kinship of humankind, is not rooted in the universal Fatherhood of God. Second, the Fatherhood of God here is potentially, rather than actually, universal. His care includes all: the reference to the sun and the rain makes that clear. But the filial relationship with God is dependent in this context on the imitation of God: 'Love . . . that you may be sons . . .' Again, as the prayer of Jesus, discussed earlier, showed, it takes two to make a relationship, even though the New Testament indicates universal goodwill on God's side.

Before we leave this passage, a word needs to be said about the concept here of the Father's perfection: 'Be perfect as your heavenly Father is perfect' (v.48).

There is an echo here of Leviticus 19.18, but the parallel in Luke (6.36) is 'be merciful as your Father is merciful'. Even if, as seems likely, Luke's version is nearer the original, we still have to ask the meaning of 'perfect' (*teleios*) in Matthew's version. As most commentators recognize, the clue lies in the context: the 'perfection' of God lies in the unrestricted, unlimited character of his loving.

What, then, can be said of the difference, if indeed there is one, between Old and New Testaments at this point? Both Testaments testify to the universal grace of God; even if that note is not always evident in the Old Testament, it is especially clear in some of the later Psalms. Both Testaments also agree that God is not the actual Father of all, in the normal usage of 'father'. In the Old Testament, especially, God's fatherly attitude 'belongs to the past, the future or the ideal'.[10] What is needed is a reciprocal response: 'The father who would wish to give his son all that a true father can bestow must be met, in his son, by the capacity and the will to receive.'[11] The difference, therefore, between the Testaments here lies not so much in what they say about God's Fatherhood, but in what they declare *has happened*. In Jesus, the Christians claimed, this reciprocity has occurred, and the ideal Father-son relationship has materialized.

The so-called parable of the Prodigal Son (Luke 15.11–32) is another important passage to be discussed here. Many regard the parable, even if edited by Luke, as deriving substantially from Jesus himself. Again, its main themes are foreshadowed in the Old Testament. Indeed, it could be argued that the Old Testament, particularly its teaching about the forgiveness of God in the prophets Hosea and Ezekiel, is more radical than this parable. In the prophets God does not wait for Israel's repentance, but helps to bring it about. But it would be a mistake to compare the parable and the prophets in this way, since the story does not enable us to determine the relationship between the son's penitence and

the father's compassion. Perhaps we should say that the
father's compassion finds practical expression when he saw
his son 'still a long way off' (v.20).

But what of the two father-son relationships described in
this parable? The opening of the parable leaves quite open, or
at least undefined, the relationship between the father and his
sons. We are told 'A man had two sons', and that is all. The
relationship of the younger with his father lies in the past
because he leaves home; it has yet to be shown what it will
become in the future. Similarly, the relationship of the older
son with his father is unknown to us until almost the end of
the story. The father is constant in his love for both (vv.20
and 31); the younger one is reinstated, and a father-son
relationship is restored (or restored at a deeper level than
before?). With the older son, something has gone wrong, or
failed to materialize in his relationship with his father, for
whom he says he has 'slaved' for so many years (v.29). What
is more, he calls his brother 'your son', implicitly disowning
any relationship between himself and his brother. In fact, it
may be correct to see in his accusation, 'This your son
devoured all your livelihood' a bitter comment by one who
resented his father's unpatriarchal conduct. His father's
house remained open to him (v.31), but to realize afresh
the potential father-son relationship for him now meant
welcoming home a prodigal. All of this needs to be related to
the context of this parable in Luke. The story is told in
response to the complaint of the Pharisees that Jesus
welcomed and ate with sinners. The story thus implies that
through the ministry of Jesus the father-son relationship
which God intended for these 'sinners' was now being
realized.

We must now recall two things from our earlier discussion.
First, I suggested that what or who a person worships will
imprint itself on that person's life. What a person is reflects
the God s/he believes in. Second, we saw how, according

to the Gospels, this was true of Jesus and the Kingdom. He exemplified it. The Kingdom of which he spoke was imprinted on his life.

This concept of 'imprint' (or 'image') is exemplified above all in the way in which father/son language is applied to a divine–human relationship. 'Like father, like son' carried even more weight in the ancient world than in ours. In particular, to say in a Jewish context that a man was the son of someone or something was to refer either to that person's origin, or his character, or his destiny (as the expressions Simon bar Jonah, 'sons of thunder', and 'son of perdition' indicate). Another filial characteristic to note in this Jewish context is *obedience*, not obedience rendered grudgingly in the spirit of a slave, but obedience given spontaneously and gladly. The theme of obedience brings us naturally to an observation, however brief, about father-son language in John's Gospel.

It is unfortunate that New Testament scholarship is so often polarized. In discussions of the teaching of Jesus one all too often finds one of two positions: either an uncritical view which assumes that everything attributed to Jesus in the Gospels was therefore spoken by him (a view which conflicts with the evidence), or a more critical view, but one which leave John's Gospel entirely out of consideration, as if no sayings in that Gospel go back to Jesus himself. It is reasonable to assume that the truth, in the case of all four Gospels, lies somewhere in between these two extremes. Two sayings, in particular, in John are similar to the father-son saying of Matt. 11.25–27. At 3.35 Jesus says: 'The Father loves the Son and has entrusted everything into his hand', and in 5.19–20a (identified by C.H. Dodd as a parable of a workshop in which the father taught his son 'everything he knew'):

> . . . the Son can do nothing by himself; he does only what he sees the Father doing; whatever the Father does, the Son

does. For the Father loves the Son and shows him all that he himself is doing . . .' (5.19b, 20a).

It is impossible to be sure where the original parable (if such it was) ends and Johannine editing begins. Indeed, the whole may have been so thoroughly edited that no clear line between the two exist anyway. We may guess that references to a 'pre-existent' Son (i.e. existing with his Father in heaven, before his coming to earth – as in John 17.5), and to the Son *glorifying* the Father (a distinctively Johannine word) are later developments, but we cannot be sure. What can be seen, however, is the inseparability of Father and Son: for example, 'the one who does not honour the Son does not honour the Father' (5.23; compare 8.19 and 14.9). The language of John is often very different from that of the other Gospels, and it is important that the distinctiveness of each Gospel be recognized. But John often makes explicit what is implicit or less prominent in the others. And this is true of the divine imprint on 'the Son'.

To summarize the arguments thus far: there is a bifurcation in Jesus' Kingdom language: sometimes the Kingdom is the subject, usually of verbs of movement (it is at hand, it has come upon you, it is coming); sometimes it features as the object of verbs, particularly of verbs of seeing, receiving and entering. There is also a distinction to be observed in Jesus' father/son language: God's Fatherhood is a *potential* relationship waiting to be realized in all people, but, infrequent though the evidence is in the Synoptic Gospels, this relationship has been actualized in Jesus. In him that father-son relationship is not a possibility; it is a reality.

Before we leave the subject of father-son language, it is important to distinguish it from patriarchal language. The two are not necessarily the same. A patriarch, so the word suggests, is male, and rules; to be male and to rule are the essence of patriarchy. By contrast, a father is a father because

he has children and, we might add, a father is a true father if
he cares for his children.

There can be little doubt that in the Bible, in both
Testaments, both kinds of language co-exist, and are sometimes confused. But Old and New Testaments alike suggest
that the basis of God's Fatherhood is covenantal; he is a
Father because he has a son (i.e. Israel), whom he loves and
cares for. This is why the image of a mother occasionally
replaces father imagery: the essence of fatherhood *in this
context* is not maleness, but a loving relationship with his
children.

We turn to a third kind of language about God in the
teaching of Jesus, the so-called 'divine passives'. An example
of such a passive occurs in Matt. 7.1, 'Do not judge, and you
will not be judged'. Here the passive voice of the verb 'will
not be judged' means 'God will not judge you' (as the Good
News Bible accurately interprets). There are many passive
verbs of this kind in the Synoptic Gospels, and what follows
comprises a brief survey of them.

As far as I am aware, Jeremias' *New Testament Theology*
remains the most recent investigation of them, and so I begin
from his list and observations.[12] However, two criticisms of
his work, careful and detailed though it is, are necessary.
First, Jeremias under-estimates the difficulty of establishing
which of these sayings go back to Jesus himself. The 'divine
passive' is to be found in Paul; the best-known example is I
Cor. 13.12b, 'Now I know in part; then I will know fully,
even as *I have been fully known*' (i.e. as God has fully known
me).

This same way of avoiding a direct reference to God by
using a passive verb can also be found in other Jewish
authors, and so we cannot assume that all divine passives
in the Gospels go back to Jesus himself. Sometimes, for
example, a divine passive occurs as an addition to a tradition
which the evangelist is following, and then it may well be a

gloss on the earlier tradition. So 'let your will be done on earth as in heaven' is widely regarded as an expansion of an earlier, shorter version of the Lord's Prayer. Similarly, from Jeremias' long list, there must be at least some doubt whether all of those sayings go back to Jesus himself. For example, Matt. 15.24 has: 'Jesus replied "I was sent [i.e. God sent me] to the lost sheep of the house of Israel, and to them alone"' (v.24). When we compare the equivalent passage in Mark (7.24–30), Matt. 15.24 looks very much like Matthew's addition to the original account by Mark. But that still leaves a good number, many of which do not look as if they have been attributed to Jesus by the early church (and many of which have parallels in one, or both, of the other Synoptic Gospels).

Second, Jeremias exaggerates the number of present divine passives; the vast majority are future. The clearest exceptions are those which refer to the destiny of the Son of Man, as in Mark 9.31, although most of these present tenses have a future sense: 'The Son of man is now to be handed over into the power of men, and they will kill him; and three days after being killed he will rise again.'

When we have made due allowance for the editorial work of the evangelists, what remains? Some sayings have a strong claim to go back to Jesus himself because they occur in more than one primary source: e.g. Mark and Q. These include Mark 4.24–25: 'He also said to them, "Take note of what you hear; the measure you give is the measure you will receive with something more besides. For those who have will be given more, and those who have not will forfeit even what they have."'

Other sayings of this kind are so cryptic that they are unlikely to have been created by the early church. They include Matt. 10.26 (with its parallel in Luke 12.2): 'So do not be afraid of them. There is nothing covered up that will not be uncovered, nothing that will not be made known.' All these enigmatic sayings have a number of clearly discernible themes.

First (because by far the most numerous), many sayings allude mysteriously, sometimes threateningly, to a future sifting or reversal. When this will happen is not stated; that it will happen is many times affirmed. Thus, the person who has and the person who has not will find their having and not having affirmed and intensified (Mark 4.15, and parallels). In this mysterious future, one will be taken, the other left (Matt. 24.40/Luke 17.34; it is not clear who is favoured and who is not); those who might reasonably have assumed they were 'in', will find themselves cast out (Matt. 8.12/Luke 13.38); to avoid such a fate, any sacrifice however drastic, should be made (Mark 9.45, 47/Matt. 5.29); no one will escape this purifying fire (Mark 9.49); the searching nature of this future test will be proportionate to what a person has been given (Luke 12.48). But it is possible, even now to escape (Luke 10.20).

Whenever, however this happens, the future will not simply rubber stamp the present status quo. There will be reversals of a revolutionary kind: the lowly will be exalted (Matt. 23.12/Luke 14.11 and 18.14); the poor and those who mourn will find comfort and blessing (Matt. 5.4/Luke 16.25 etc.)

Several sayings reflect what the Jewish scholar Solomon Schechter called 'measure for measure': for example, 'Judge and you *will not be judged*', 'Be merciful, and *mercy will be shown to you*'. There are many Old Testament and later Jewish antecedents for this particular kind of saying. As for the underlying theology, the warning about judgment reflects the conviction, expressed in Wisd. 11.16: '. . . the instruments of someone's sin are the instruments of his punishment'.

Several examples of this kind can be given from rabbinic writings and from the Pseudepigrapha. Although the sayings sound retaliatory, they are best understood as examples of evil-doers creating their own evil destiny.

Such retribution, or punishment, might be spiritual, rather than physical: for example, 'the reward of a command is a command, and the reward of a transgression is a transgression'. Thus, 'if a man takes the initiative in holiness, even though in a small way, Heaven will help him to reach it in a much higher degree'.[13]

It would be wrong to give the impression, however, that all the so-called divine passives in the sayings of Jesus are to do with retribution and future judgment. That is clearly not so. There are several sayings which denote the generosity of God. Thus disciples are told, 'Ask and it will be given to you, seek and you will find, knock and it will be opened to you' (Matt. 7.7/Luke 11.9). Similarly, those who seek the Kingdom will receive all they need and more (Matt. 6.33); those who now hunger and thirst to see God's justice prevail will be satisfied; those who mourn will be comforted (Matt. 5.6,4). Perhaps the most striking of these sayings expressing divine bounty is sandwiched between other 'divine passive' sayings, reflecting the 'measure for measure' principle to which we have just referred. Thus at Luke 6.38 (after 'Do not judge . . .' and before 'Whatever measure you deal out to others . . .') we have: 'Give, and gifts will be given to you. Good measure, pressed and shaken down and running over, will be poured into your lap.'

In the divine passive sayings which refer to a future judgment, whether as confirmation of, or retribution for, or overturning of what is now the case, we find the obverse side of the potential revealed in the sayings about a Kingdom and a Father. The Kingdom is a reality, but people may fail to see it, may choose not to enter it, may refuse to do what is required to share in it. The heavenly Father *is*. But 'Father' here is a *relational* concept; a 'father', by definition, has children. In New Testament terms, God is a person's Father if that person becomes God's 'son'. The fundamental concepts of God's kingship, with its corollary of life, and God's Fatherhood, with its corollary of 'sonship', point to the potentiality of human beings. Some of the divine passive sayings indicate how much is at stake in present attitudes and decisions.

But even when we have explored every reference to God in the sayings of Jesus, or in teaching attributed to Jesus, we still have only one side of the equation. What of Jesus as God's Son?

Again, New Testament scholarship has polarized unhelpfully. Some adopt a somewhat uncritical approach ('of course Jesus thought of himself as the Son of God'), whilst others adopt an unduly sceptical approach, rejecting all references to Jesus' sonship as early church creations. There are good grounds for believing that Jesus spoke of himself, however infrequently, as a son, or the Son. (Indeed, this would be the natural corollary of addressing God as his Father.) Apart from Matt. 11.25–27, there is the cryptic Mark 13.32 (by attributing ignorance to the Son, this saying at least passes the criterion of 'embarrassment'),[14] the parable of the wicked husbandmen (Mark 12.1–11 and parallels) and, however mythological the accounts, the baptism and transfiguration.

Whatever Jesus himself thought, and whether he referred to himself frequently or infrequently as God's Son, the testimony of the New Testament is that in some way he was God's Son. And therefore we need to ask what was conveyed by Jesus' life in its entirety. In particular, what light is shed on 'the Father' of whom Jesus spoke by what is implied or claimed about Jesus as his Son? After all, teachers teach not only by what they say, but by what they are and do.

We may begin by asking what the Synoptic Gospels mean by referring to Jesus as God's Son.

Earlier we noted that the expression 'son of' might denote a man's origin, character or destiny. In the first three Gospels (unlike John), very little is made of the 'origin' theme with reference to Jesus' birth. Only Luke 1.35 makes an explicit connection between Jesus' sonship and his origin: 'The angel answered her (i.e. Mary) "The Holy Spirit will come upon you, and the power of the Most High will overshadow you; for that reason the holy child to be born will be called Son of God."'

Even in Matthew, the only other Gospel which utilizes the (relatively early?) tradition about the virgin birth, no connection is made between the manner of his conception and his Sonship.

How is this to be explained? The answer is to be found in the history and the associations of 'son of God' in Jewish tradition, including the Old Testament. 'Son of God', first and foremost, referred to Israel:

When Israel was a child, I loved him,
and out of Egypt I called my son (Hos. 11.1).

It referred also to kings of Israel. 'He said to me, "You are my son; today I have begotten you"' (Ps. 2.7). Of course, the idea of origin is present in both these verses. But here origin means the calling or election of Israel, or the coronation of Israel's king. These themes may be implied, or taken for granted, in many of the Gospel traditions. But so, too, it is argued here, is the theme of character, that is, the 'divine imprint' on the life of Jesus.

But there is more to be said. Jesus was the supreme exemplar of his own teaching. Firm evidence for this assertion can be found when we examine the Gospel sayings about the Kingdom of God, and compare them with what is said or implied about Jesus either in the Gospels or elsewhere in the New Testament. A few examples from Matthew and Luke must suffice. (There are very few Kingdom sayings in Mark which are not in Matthew or Luke – examples are 4.26 and 12.34.)

If we begin with Matthew's version of the beatitudes, it is not too far-fetched to assume that early Christians would have seen a profile of Jesus in these sayings: 'gentle' (compare Matt. 11.29 and 21.5), 'merciful', 'pure in heart', 'peace-maker' 'persecuted for righteousness' sake' – all these cohere with New Testament portraits or understandings of Jesus. It is reasonable, then, to suppose that the same is true of the first beatitude (literally) 'Happy are the poor in spirit; for the Kingdom of Heaven is theirs.' Behind this saying almost certainly lies the Hebrew word *ani*, meaning, originally, 'poor' and coming to mean 'devout'. Whether this double meaning of 'poor' lies behind Luke's form of the first beatitude ('Happy are you poor' 6.20), is impossible to say. But several texts in the Gospels indicate the material poverty of Jesus, for example, 'The Son of Man has nowhere to lay his head' (Matt. 8.20/Luke 9.59).

Other sayings also fit Jesus. The Gospels portray a man who 'sought first the Kingdom' (Matt. 6.33), whose child-like humility and abandonment of wealth' (Matt. 18.1–4, 19.23–4) fulfilled two of the requirements for 'entry' into the Kingdom. And, finally, the saying 'the one who is least in the Kingdom of heaven is greater than John (Matt. 11.11; cf. Luke 7.28) is probably a self-reference which, if understood in this way, is a striking example of the humility of Jesus. The description of John as 'born of woman' needs to be borne in mind, and compared with the reply of Jesus to Nicodemus: 'Jesus answered, "In very truth I tell you, no-one can see the Kingdom of God unless he has been born again"' (John 3.3; cf. v.5).

But it is not enough to say 'Jesus practised what he preached'. The theological implications of this must be explored. If, as we have contended, 'the Kingdom' means God himself, then to put into effect the message of the Kingdom is to reflect the character and being of God.

The first three Gospels give expression to this in many

ways. Even if we set aside for a moment the 'canopy' which Matthew places over his Gospel, by the references at 1.23 (explicit) and 28.20 (implicit) to Jesus as 'God with us', there are many other clues that Jesus bears the divine imprint. Three examples may be given.

First, Jesus fulfils the 'profile' of a king of Israel. He is 'the Son of David' not, of course, in all the ways which his contemporaries expected him to be, but rather as one who does what God does. The king, after all, was God's viceroy, and, as such, was the executor of God's 'policies', as Psalm 72 clearly shows:

> God, endow the king with your own justice, his royal person with your righteousness, that he may govern your people rightly and deal justly with your oppressed ones. May hills and mountains provide your people with prosperity in righteousness. May he give judgment for the oppressed among the people and help to the needy; may he crush the oppressor (1–4).

> For he will rescue the needy who appeal for help, the distressed who have no protector. He will have pity on the poor and the needy, and deliver the needy from death; he will redeem them from oppression and violence and their blood will be precious in his eyes (12–14).

So, just as the king, by what he did, not least for the poor, bore what I am calling 'the divine imprint', so did Jesus, as the compassionate 'Son of David'. There is a hint of this in the way in which a healing story immediately precedes the so-called 'triumphal entry', both of which feature this Davidic theme (Mark 10.46–11.11; Matt. 20.29 – 21.11).

Second, we need to recall our earlier observation that in the ancient world the maxim 'like father, like son', was a very weighty one. With this maxim in mind, references to 'sons of

God' take on extra meaning. The most important occurs in the passage already discussed (Matt. 5.43–48), where it is clear that the family resemblance, as it were, lies in embracing even the enemy and the persecutor with love and prayer. Luke 23.34, the prayer of Jesus for those who crucified him (Jews or Romans, or both?), illustrates this with: 'Jesus said "Father, forgive them; they do not know what they are doing." '[15]

Another verse in the Sermon on the Mount describes 'sons of God' as peacemakers (Matt. 5.9). If our line of argument is correct, it follows that this too may be said both of Jesus, and of God. There is much in the Bible to support this interpretation, not least the conviction shared by several New Testament writers, that God in Christ 'made peace' between Jew and Gentile (see especially Eph. 2.14–16). Such peace, however, is not easily attained, and often lies on the far side of conflict: 'Do you think that I have come to bring peace to the earth? No, I tell you, but rather division!' (Luke 12.51; cf. Matt. 10.34).

It is important, in exploring this theme of 'like father, like son', not to confine the scope of the exploration only to those passages where there are explicit references to it. Assumptions universally held in a culture or society do not always need to be spelt out, though they will naturally be made explicit from time to time, as in the second century (BC) writing of Ben Sirach:

Be a father to the fatherless,
and as a husband to widows,
and God shall call you his son (Ecclus. 4.10).

A third example of the 'divine imprint' on 'the Son of God' is less obvious but no less important. The four Gospels vary in both the frequency and the ways in which they refer to the anger and the sorrow of Jesus. Luke, for example, seems to omit all the explicit references in Mark to Jesus' anger. For example, in the story of Jesus and the Children, where Mark has '. . . but when Jesus saw it he was indignant, and said to them "Let the children come to me, do not try to stop them; for the Kingdom of God belongs to such as these"' (Mark 10.14) Luke has: 'But Jesus called for the children and said, "Let the children come to me; do not try to stop them, for the Kingdom of God belongs to such as these"' (Luke 18.16).

The Old Testament allusions or echoes, however, show that the evangelists see in the anger and sorrow of Jesus the divine anger and sorrow. Thus the words of Jesus in Mark 9.19, 'You faithless generation . . .' appear to echo the words of God in Deut. 32.20:

. . . they are a perverse generation,
children in whom there is no faithfulness.

Similarly, the tears of Jesus over Jerusalem (Luke 19.41) recall the sorrow of the prophet Jeremiah, as he speaks for God:

My joy is gone, grief is upon me, my heart is sick.
Hark, the cry of my poor people . . .
The harvest is past, the summer is ended,
and we are not saved (Jer. 8.18, 19a, 20).

In sum, there is a great deal of material in the first three Gospels which illustrate the theme 'like father, like son'. By what is said of 'sons of God' in general, and of Jesus, *the* Son of God, the evangelists point up the divine imprint on his life. His calling and election (i.e. origin) are, of course, fundamental, even where they are not explicitly referred to. So, too, is his character: in his Davidic role, as the one who befriends the poor, as the one who loves even the enemy, and the one who responds with both anger and sorrow to Israel's 'hardness of heart', he reflects the character of the Father.

The theme of Jesus' destiny must await the next chapter, since it relates particularly to his resurrection. In this chapter we turn, finally and briefly, to the third of the approaches outlined at the beginning, the synthesizing approach of putting together what different New Testament writers have to say about Jesus and God. Here we are concerned with placing the testimony of John alongside that of the first three Gospels.

The very difference of John from the other Gospels means that in much New Testament study the four Gospels are rarely brought together. Indeed, it is sometimes a spoken or unspoken axiom of New Testament scholarship that 'never the twain – i.e. the Synoptics and John – should meet'. This question of method highlights the difficulty of determining both the limits and the possibilities of an enquiry about 'Jesus and his God'. Is this just an historical enquiry? And what would that mean anyway? What would count as evidence? How does anyone discover in depth the religious experience of another?

No historical writing is entirely objective; no interpretation of any text, religious or otherwise, can be entirely objective. So what we do with John's Gospel, whether we include or exclude it from our enquiry, involves historical and theological judgments. I am suggesting that we should relate the synoptics and John, not primarily because they are manifestly about the same person (that argument would presumably require us to explore the non-canonical gospels as well). Rather, the four Gospels need to be brought together for two underlying theological reasons:

1. The relatedness of the Synoptics and John has a theological or spiritual dimension, as well as an historical and literary one. The four Gospels are united in a common religious tradition, and it can be argued that a fuller meaning of the Bible is realizable only in dialogue with that tradition.

2. A good case can be made for the view of Clement of

Alexandria that John is 'the spiritual gospel', provided we are clear what we mean by that slippery expression. The father/son language of that Gospel is best understood as making more explicit what was implicit in the earlier Gospels. Or, to put it another way, John articulates the relationship which was remembered, or perceived to exist, between Jesus and his God. In the synoptic tradition father-son language is preserved, not plentifully, but suggestively and significantly. In John it is developed in a way which makes this Gospel a spiritual commentary on the earlier traditions. Here the motif of the divine imprint on a human life is given its fullest and deepest treatment. All three aspects of sonship – origin, character, destiny – are highlighted repeatedly: where Jesus has come from, who has sent him, whom he reflects, and to whom he returns, are all major Johannine themes. So at the heart of the question of God, according to the New Testament, is the inseparability of the Father and the Son:

'The one who does not honour the Son does not honour the Father' (John 5.23).

'If you had known me, you would have known my Father as well' (John 8.19).

'Do you not believe that I am in the Father, and the Father is in me?' (John 14.10).

'The Father and I are one' (John 10.30).

Here in more explicit form, is the theme of the divine imprint:

'Anyone who has seen me has seen the Father' (John 14.9).

In more philosophical terms, we need to stand Feuerbach on his head, and say 'Theology *includes* anthropology'. The biblical story begins with the claim that God made humankind in his own image, and began, not just with a command, but with an invitation and a search, '(Adam), where are you?' (Gen. 3.9). So Jesus and his God are the realization of the father/son relationship adumbrated in the creation narratives. In the language of the leading theme of this book, at the heart of New Testament teaching about God lies the claim that the divine imprint is seen most clearly in Jesus of Nazareth.

2

The Crucified God

In chapter 1 I outlined a three-fold approach to our subject:

1. A linguistic one: how do New Testament writers use language about God?
2. A 'theology from below' – what can be said about God from the 'divine imprint' on two people in particular, Jesus and Paul.
3. A synthesizing approach: how may we relate what different writers in the New Testament have to say?

Following the first approach, I suggested that the 'Kingdom' sayings of the Gospels can be subdivided: when 'the Kingdom' is the subject, it refers to God himself in his self-revelation, and when 'the Kingdom' is the object, as in the expression 'entering the Kingdom', it may be (and sometimes is), replaced by the word 'life', since that is what it means.

The word 'Father', as a term for God, though infrequent in the first three Gospels (apart from the Sermon on the Mount), is a distinctive, and crucially important, *relational* term: a 'father' implies children, and a person, in relating to God as Father, thereby becomes God's 'son' ('daughter'), and thus enters into life.

The so-called 'divine passives' comprised a third linguistic category in the teaching of Jesus. Some of these sayings, often allusive and cryptic, point to the divine generosity. Others, and these are more plentiful, allude to a future sifting, highlighting how much is at stake in the offer of 'the Kingdom', and the potential relationship with the Father.

The second approach to our subject was to look at those texts, which referred to 'sons of God', and at the portrait of Jesus as God's Son, so that on the principle of 'like father, like son', we might discover what such a son, or sons, implied about the character of their Father. In the case of Jesus, it was suggested that as the Son of David, particularly in his concern for the poor and oppressed, he acted as God's viceroy, doing what God does. Other references to 'children' or 'sons' of God (Matt. 5.9 and 5.45) suggested that to be a peacemaker and to embrace the enemy is to be like God. The anger and sorrow of Jesus also reflected the anger and sorrow of God.

Thirdly, John's Gospel makes explicit the Father-Son relationship, including the divine imprint on Jesus, which is implicit in the other three Gospels. The underlying connection comes to expression in the text 'The one who has seen me has seen the Father' (John 14.9).

In this chapter we examine the relationship of the message of Jesus to the message of Paul about God. But first the picture needs to be broadened by means of a brief sketch of language about God as it was used by Jewish contemporaries, or near-contemporaries, of Jesus and Paul.

The literature is very varied, even within this short compass of time. Wisdom literature is represented by the Wisdom of Solomon, apocalyptic literature by I Enoch, IV Ezra (and, rather later, II Baruch), there are the Psalms of Solomon, the long discourses of Philo, the varied literature of the Qumran community, to say nothing of the rabbinic literature, some traditions within which no doubt go back to the time of Jesus and Paul.[1]

When we examine this literature's language about God, certain features stand out.

1. The language of *particularity*. By this is meant language reflecting the conviction that God had called or chosen one

particular nation, Israel, and that the land of Israel was in some way God's land in a way that other land was not. Such language is to be found even in the Wisdom of Solomon which otherwise has some very inclusive-sounding theology. The writer has apparently borrowed the language of Greek philosophy (notably at 7.22ff.) to describe Wisdom, and express a universal kind of theology in, for example, the following statements: 'You have mercy on all, because you can do all things, and you overlook men's sins in order to bring them to repentance' (12.15). 'But you are just, and you order all things justly, counting it alien to your power to condemn anyone to undeserved punishment' (12.15).

But, alongside this apparent inclusiveness, we find a strong strand of particularism, as in the reference to the land of Israel at 12.7 as 'the land most precious of all to you'. This particularism comes through especially strongly in the later chapters, narrating the story of the Exodus, the writer has this to say of the Egyptians:

> For their enemies deserved to be deprived of light and
> imprisoned in darkness,
> those who had kept your children imprisoned,
> through whom the imperishable light of the law was to be
> given to the world.
> When they had resolved to kill the infants of your holy
> ones . . . .
> you in punishment took away a multitude of their children
> . . . .' (Wisd. 18.4–5).

What is said, again and again, is that the people of God gain *at others' expense*. Thus God rescues the Israelites only by punishing the Egyptians: 'For by the same means whereby you punished our antagonists you summoned us to your side and glorified us' (18.8).

2. The language of *crisis* and the search for a *theodicy* (i.e.

in this instance, attempting to explain why God allows his chosen people to suffer). This is particularly apparent in the Psalms of Solomon, in the Enochic literature, some of which at least was written against a background of oppression, and in other apocalyptic such as IV Ezra and II Baruch. The root cause was the deepening crisis in Palestine in the first century AD, culminating in two Jewish-Roman wars (AD 66–70 and AD 132–5). This was an economic, as well as a political crisis. But it had an acute religious dimension, since at its heart was the question 'Why do the wicked prosper and the righteous suffer?' For the author(s) of the Psalms of Solomon, the crisis centred on the status and vindication of God's chosen people. (Not surprisingly, there are many references in the Psalms to the 'judgments' or 'judging' activity of God.) Because the writer believes that God rewards the righteous and punishes the wicked, and because he believes in Israel's special status as God's covenant people, he struggles to reconcile theology with reality. Two verses, in particular, express the writer's anguish: 'Discipline us as you wish, but do not turn (us) over to the Gentiles' (Ps. 7.3), and 'Do not neglect us, our God, lest the Gentiles devour us as if there were no redeemer' (Ps. 8.30). The other writings mentioned here reflect the same questioning: how can the God of Israel allow this to happen to Israel?

3. The language of *grace*. Since the seminal work of E. P. Sanders[2] we have learned not to label Judaism as legalistic, as if all Jews believed in 'salvation by works'. To those who thought or think in this way, the language of some of the Qumran hymns, from the Dead Sea Scrolls, must be surprising:

By Thy goodness alone is man righteous,
and with Thy many mercies Thou strengthenest him
(from Hymn XIII).

> And I know that man is not righteous
> except through Thee (from Hymn XVI).

> For to God belongs my justification,
> and the perfection of my way (from IQS 11.26).[3]

Paul himself could surely have written these words! Yet there is an important difference in the language of grace used in the Qumran literature, and that used by Paul. The difference is the product of a different theology and a different context. At Qumran the language of grace is primarily the language of predestination: the elect are the elect, and *will remain so*, and, conversely, the wicked are the wicked *and will remain so*, e.g. IQH 4.38 'Thou . . . hast created the just and the wicked.' The elect are who they are by the grace of God, but they are a tightly knit group (their locus of revelation being the scriptures). Whilst Paul and his interpreters in the New Testament sometimes seem to express, or reflect, similar views, there can be no doubt that in the New Testament view, all can be saved. Such, at least, is God's will: for example, 'this is right and acceptable in the sight of God our Saviour, who desires everyone to be saved and come to the knowledge of the truth' (I Tim. 2.3–4).

When Paul's language about God is compared with that of all his Jewish contemporaries, except Jesus, it is clear that there is a new locus of revelation. This is seen very clearly in the contrast between Paul's credal summary in I Cor. 8.6:

> . . . for us there is one God, the Father,
> . . . and one Lord, Jesus Christ . . .

and two similar summaries in Josephus, the Jewish historian who was Paul's near-contemporary:

> '. . . one God and one race of the Jews' (*Hebraion*) and
> 'one temple of one God . . .'[4]

It seems, from these parallels, that 'the Lord Jesus Christ' has displaced both Israel and the Temple. Or are we to say: has fulfilled the destinies or roles of Israel and the Temple?

But we are only at the beginning of our inquiry. The most obvious linguistic result of this in Paul's writings is what James Dunn has called the 'interplay' between expressions about God and expressions about Christ. When these are examined more closely, it is clear that the focus can be identified more precisely. The focus is: what took place *between God and Jesus in the cross and resurrection*.

I begin with an observation about a fundamental feature of Paul's language about God: God is the author and destiny of all things. Paul usually expresses this by prepositions: in I Cor. 8.6 by 'from' (*'ex'*) and 'for' (*'eis'*). Similarly, when we turn to statements about the cross and resurrection, we find God is almost always the subject: *God* sent, *God* handed over, *God* raised . . .

'In the fullness of time, God sent his Son, born of a woman . . .' (Gal. 4.4).

'God sent his Son in the likeness of the flesh of sin' (Rom. 8.3).

'He who did not spare his own Son but gave him up for us all' (Rom. 8.33).

As for Paul's language about the resurrection, it is almost always God-centred: either Paul says '*God* raised . . .' or 'Christ was raised/is risen' (where the verb is the so-called divine passive, meaning 'was raised *by God*'). I Thess. 4.14 seems to be the only variant to this pattern in Paul's letters: 'For since we believe that Jesus died and rose again, even so through Jesus God will bring with him those who have died.'

What is not immediately clear from I Cor. 8.6 is the relationship between God and Jesus. 'One God' and 'one Lord' are simply placed side by side; their relationship is not spelt out. To put this another way, explicit statements (*implied* references in Paul are another matter) to what we have come to call the divinity of Christ and the incarnation are few and far between. Some scholars question whether there are any at all. This does not mean Paul did not believe in the realities which these later doctrines attempted to express. It means that he expressed himself differently, or that such matters were not an issue for him in the way that they were for later generations.

Let us take a moment to explore this further. Paul nowhere calls Jesus God in so many words, unless he does so at Rom. 9.5 ('. . . from them . . . comes the messiah who is over all, God blessed for ever. Amen') but in this instance it depends on how the sentence is punctuated.[5] The greeting with which he begins most of his letters, 'Grace to you and peace from God our Father and the Lord Jesus Christ . . .', shows that he *associates* Jesus closely with God. Some of his 'Lord' language points the same way: Rom. 10.13, a quotation from the book of Joel, could be a reference to God or to Jesus as 'the Lord': 'For "everyone who calls on the name of the Lord shall be saved".' So, although the words 'God' and 'the Lord' are by no means interchangeable, there is some overlap: 'the Lord' serves *both* to differentiate Jesus from God, *and* to associate him with God (as in I Cor. 8.6).

The question of Christ's so-called 'pre-existence' is a more complicated matter.

The Old Testament and later Jewish writings have several examples of 'pre-existence' language, describing how 'wisdom' or 'the Law' were with God before creation. So in Prov. 8.23 divine wisdom says

I was formed in earliest times,
at the beginning, before earth itself.

And from the rabbinic writings, we have a saying which no doubt reflects the conviction that these things transcended, in their ultimate importance, everything in the created order:

'Seven things were created before the world was created –
Torah, repentance, the Garden of Eden, Gehinnon, the
throne of glory, the temple, and the name of the Messiah.'

As James Dunn has pointed out, the conviction that somehow Christ 'pre-existed' his earthly life underlies, or precedes, incarnational language (we don't say someone *became*
a human being unless that someone already existed). But in
this respect Paul's language is usually ambiguous. II Cor. 8.9
('the Lord Jesus [Christ] who was rich, yet for your sakes
became poor) may be a reference to the incarnation, but it
could allude to the cross.

Similarly, the hymn of Phil. 2.6–11 may give an extended
contrast between Adam and Christ ('he, being in the *image* of
God . . .') or, as most translations have it, it may be an early
reference to the incarnation:

> who, though he was in the form of God,
> did not regard equality with God as something to be
> exploited,
> but emptied himself, taking the form of a slave,
> being born in human likeness.
> And being found in human form,
> he humbled himself
> and became obedient to the point of death –
> even death on a cross.

The precise meaning of this poetic language continues to be
hotly debated by scholars. But many commentators now
think that the poem is comparing and contrasting Jesus with
Adam, and therefore may not be, as has been traditionally
thought, incarnational language.

As for I Cor. 8.6, the meaning here depends on what 'all
things' refers to in the second part of the creed: 'Yet for us
there is one God, the Father, from whom are all things and
for whom we exist, and one Lord Jesus Christ, through

whom (are) all things and through whom we exist.' Surprising as it may sound, the precise meaning of 'all things' in Paul varies according to context. It may refer to 'creation', as in the first part of this verse; it may refer to our salvation, as it clearly does in II Cor. 5.18: 'All this is from God who reconciled us to himself through Christ, and has given us the ministry of reconciliation.'

As for incarnational language, the nearest we come to this in the letters bearing Paul's name[6] (apart from Phil. 2.6) are Col. 1.19 'For in him God in his fullness chose to dwell . . .' and Col. 2.9: 'For it is in Christ that the Godhead in all its fullness dwells embodied . . .'[7]

To sum up this part of the argument, the precise relationship between God and Jesus is rarely the focus of Paul's attention. (Even references to 'Father' and 'Son' are rare, and what such a father-son relationship means is not spelt out in the way that it is in John's Gospel.) So, if we read Paul's language about God and Jesus without, so to speak, the benefit of hindsight – that is, not through the spectacles of later Christian doctrine – there is something of a gap: 'God sent . . . God raised . . .', but where was God in between?

It is not immediately apparent from Paul's writings that we should speak of the crucified *God*. The divine initiative in sending Christ is clear, the divine power in raising Christ is frequently mentioned. One can perhaps see why Gnosticism filled the apparent gap in its own distinctive way: God was there at the beginning, and at the end, but he by-passed the cross in between. We are back with our question: what happened between God and Jesus in the crucifixion?

It is at this point that we must turn to what Paul says about himself, particularly in the letters to Corinth. It is clear from both letters that his apostolic credentials and lifestyle were questioned and criticized. The details need not delay us: suffice to say that Paul did not match up to what the Corinthians thought an apostle should be. They were not impressed by his appearance or his eloquence: 'For they say "his letters are weighty and strong but his bodily presence is weak, and his speech contemptible"' (II Cor. 10.10). And whatever his 'thorn in the flesh' (II Cor. 12.7–10), a sick apostle was for them a 'contradiction in terms' (C. K. Barrett). They couldn't understand why he insisted on earning his own keep (I Cor. 9.1–18). And, above all, they found it difficult to see in a life of constant humiliations, setbacks and sufferings, the signs of an apostle.

Paul's self-defence is to be found chiefly in four passages. It is impossible to look at them all in detail, but we shall note the salient features.

In I Cor. 4.9–13, after a sarcastic outburst at Corinthian pretensions, Paul declares: 'God has made us apostles the last act in the show, like men condemned to death in the arena, a spectacle to the whole universe – to angels as well as men' (v. 9). He continues by echoing language he has used earlier of the crucified Christ: 'We are fools for Christ . . . we are weak' (v.10). Compare 'the folly of God is wiser than human wisdom, and the weakness of God stronger than human strength' (1.25).

Another of Paul's self descriptions (II Cor. 6.3–10), also echoes language which he uses elsewhere of Christ: 'Dying we still live on . . . poor ourselves we bring wealth to many . . .' reflects the relationship between God and Christ (see II Cor. 8.9). The same is true of the passage about Paul's thorn in the flesh (II Cor. 12.1–10) and especially vv.7–10). Again, language reminiscent of the cross and resurrection is used: 'My grace is all you need: power is most fully seen in weakness' (v.9). II Cor. 4.7–12, however, has the most vivid language of this kind. What happens outwardly to the apostle, says Paul, belies inward reality: '. . . we have only earthenware jars to hold this treasure, and this proves that such transcendent power does not come from us; it is God's alone'. After describing, in a series of paired, but contrasting words, the apostle's Jack-in-a-box-like life ('We are hard-pressed but never cornered . . .' (vv.8–9)) he goes on: '*Always* we carry with us in our body the dying (*nekrosin*) of Jesus, so that in this body also the life that Jesus lives may be revealed' (v.10).

The use of *necrosin* here is remarkable: the very process of dying (cf. Rom. 8.36: 'We are being done to death for your sake all day long'). So, too, is the use of the simple name 'Jesus', occurring here four times in the space of two verses.

Verse 11 expresses slightly differently the powerful statement of v.10: '*Always* whilst still in life we are being handed over to death, because of Jesus, so that the life of Jesus may also be revealed in this mortal flesh (*sarki*) of ours'

It is very clear that these four passages are graphic examples of what Paul says elsewhere to the Corinthians: 'Imitate me as *I imitate Christ*' (I Cor. 11.1).

But what of Christ's relation to God? The answer is supplied by Paul in language which fits the context: the apostles (or Christians in general?) are being 'changed from glory into glory' (II Cor. 3.18), a glory which they receive from 'the Lord'. But this same Christ, says Paul, 'is the image of God' (II Cor. 4.4–6).

The sequence then is this: the apostle imitates, or reflects, the crucified Christ; Christ is the image of God.

In his book *Cracks in an Earthen Vessel*,[8] John T. Fitzgerald examines the passages which we have just surveyed. He calls them 'catalogues of hardships'. With reference to II Cor. 4.7–12 he comments that the participles of vv.8–9, five of which are passive, imply the connection of God with Paul's sufferings – for example, 'not abandoned'. All this, says Fitzgerald, is explicable only in the light of the cross: 'God's action *vis à vis* Paul is consonant with his action in Christ' (p.176). Fitzgerald concludes his study (p.207) by suggesting that these 'catalogues of hardships' take us not only to the centre of Paul's self-understanding, but also to the centre of his understanding of God.

So, I am suggesting, the apostle bears the imprint in his life of the crucified God: he imitates the Christ who is the image of God.

This picture can be filled out a little more by reference to another major theme in Paul's writings. Commentators have long struggled over the correct words to describe Paul's understanding of what later generations called 'the Atonement'. Does Paul use the language of sacrifice? In the broad sense, yes: Christ died 'for us'/'for our sins' (e.g. Rom. 5.8, I Cor. 15.3). But, if so, what sacrifices was he thinking of? Does the concept of substitution express Paul's understanding of the work of Christ? Both 'sacrifice' and 'substitution' beg a number of questions, but there can be little doubt that Paul *does* use the language of exchange.

Several examples can be given:

'Remember the grace of our Lord Jesus who was rich, yet for your sakes became poor, that you through his poverty might become rich' (II Cor. 8.9).

'Christ brought us freedom from the curse of the Law by coming under the curse for our sake (Gal. 3.13).

'God sent his Son . . . born under the law, to buy freedom for those who were under the law, in order that we might attain the status of sons' (Gal. 4.4–5).

In all these verses, and others (Rom. 8.3–4, II Cor. 5.21), Paul gives expression to the conviction fundamental to the theology of later church fathers: he became what we are, that we might become what he is. This is what is meant by 'interchange'.

Morna Hooker has pointed out that this pattern of exchange seems to have been the foundation of Paul's own ministry, particularly as he expresses it in I Cor. 9.19–23: 'Free from all, I make myself a slave to all, that I might save many. To Jews I behaved like a Jew to win Jews . . . To win those outside that law I behaved as if outside that law. All this I do for the sake of the gospel, that I might be' – and here Professor Hooker, rightly, I think, re-translates – 'one who participates in the work of the gospel'.[9]

Paul does not mean, as the REB and other translations have it, that he did this in order to share in the gospel's blessings – as if his entire ministry were motivated by self-interest. He means: *only* by living in this way could he be a faithful representative of that gospel or, in the terms of our argument, only thus could his ministry reflect the divine imprint.

I have spent some time exploring the 'cruciform' existence of the apostle Paul, because in this respect the apostle was an icon of the crucified God. Just as God was present in the sufferings and death of Christ, making Christ's weakness the means whereby divine power might be revealed, so the sufferings of the apostle, Paul's self-descriptions imply, are the means whereby the life and power of God may be revealed.

If we take the verb 'to hand over' as a fundamental verb in New Testament theology, we are faced with a paradox in the statement: 'God handed over his Son for us all' (Rom. 8.33). Although it is implicit, as I have argued, not explicit in Paul, the logic of his theological grammar, including his own self-descriptions, is that God handed over God to suffering and to death; that is, God placed himself on both sides of the divide which may be variously described as heaven and earth, life and death, Spirit and flesh, Spirit and Law, righteousness and wrath. This is one reason, though not the only one, why penal substitution is an inaccurate concept for describing Paul's understanding of Christ's saving work. We are nearer the mark in observing that Paul describes bearing one another's burdens as the fulfilment of the law of Christ (Gal. 6.2). It is the law of exchange which, Paul's language implies, derives from God's own life and being.

So far I have paid little attention to what Paul says about the resurrection, but it is important that it is placed alongside Paul's language about the cross, so that each may be interpreted in the light of the other.

It would be difficult to exaggerate the importance of the resurrection. God is now defined, so to speak, not as the God who brought Israel up out of Egypt, although that remained true, and an important means of interpreting this 'new thing' done by God, but as the God who raised Jesus from the dead. The range of language used in the New Testament is not great. God is almost always the subject, Jesus the object: 'God raised Jesus'. But what significance is to be attached to this?

Of several themes which might be mentioned (e.g. hope, rescue, justification), I single out one: the language of creation. Rom. 4.17 makes the connection most explicitly: '. . . in the presence of God, the God who makes the dead live and calls into being things that are not, Abraham had faith'. The creator God and the God who makes the dead live is one and the same: the language of 'new creation' is also used of those who through faith and baptism have been incorporated into the death and resurrection of Christ: 'So if anyone is in Christ, there is a new creation: everything old has passed away; see, everything has become new!' (II Cor. 5.17).

The New Testament itself requires that we put together these two kinds of language, of 'handing over' or 'exchange', referring to the cross, and of creation, referring to the resurrection. They are to be connected because the cross is never interpreted apart from the resurrection, nor the resurrection apart from the cross. Taken together, these two kinds of language suggest that God's creativity is to be found in, or emerges out of, his sharing of himself or, in biblical language, the surrender of the Son by the Father to weakness, suffering and death. And the effect of God's creation (in the New Testament, as in Gen. 1–2) is life, light and judgment (which, in biblical imagery, may be thought of as the separation of light and darkness, as it is in John 3.19): '. . . and this is the judgment, that the light has come into the world, and people loved darkness rather than light because their deeds were evil'.

It is time to return to I Cor. 8.6, and to observe the personal pronouns in this credal summary:

> For us (there is) one God the Father
>> from whom are all things and *we* for him
> And one Lord Jesus Christ
>> through whom are all things and *we* through him'

There are several questions here. First, what is the meaning of 'all things'? Does it mean 'creation'? That is possible, but as we noted earlier in this chapter, the word 'all' can change its meaning in Paul, according to its context. In II Cor. 5.18, it may mean something like 'the whole work of salvation'. So it is possible that, here in I Cor. 8.6, the first 'all things' refers to God's work in creation, and the second to God's work in redemption 'through' our Lord Jesus Christ. This is not only possible, but probable since 'through' applied to Christ in Paul always refers to his agency in salvation. But if that is so, what is being said about 'the Father'? Here the 'for us' must be given due weight. Paul is talking about Christian experience and conviction, not universal religious truths. So even though 'one God the Father' might resemble, in language and theology, what a Greek might say about Zeus, the context means, and Paul's use of the word elsewhere reinforces this, that 'Father' must be given its full Christian content. So the creed should not be divided into a statement about creation ('We believe in God' etc.) and a statement about redemption ('one Lord Jesus Christ'). This, rather, is a credal summary of the *Christian experience of God* (admittedly, without a reference to the Holy Spirit, though this is *implied* in the light of Paul's theology as a whole).

The final clause 'we through him' is the phrase which cryptically summarizes *how* 'we' find, or receive, 'new creation'. The process is spelt out most fully in Rom. 6.1–11, which describes how a convert is immersed in a cruciform existence. For example, 'We know that our old self was crucified with him so that the body of sin might be destroyed, and we might no longer be enslaved to sin' (v.6). 'Immersed' is probably the right word, since these verses probably expound the meaning of baptism (cf. Gal. 2.19–21, 6.14).

What is common to all these passages is the description of a profound re-orientation of a person's whole existence, so much so that 'dying' and 'rising' and 'new creation' are appropriate images for it.

How does all this relate to the question of God, which is our subject? The answer lies, again, in the inseparability of the Fatherhood of God, and sonship. It is noteworthy that 'Father' in Paul's writings is supremely a doxological word. It occurs very rarely outside the opening greetings of the letters, or outside a context which is not explicitly or implicitly prayerful or doxological. So we have, for example, 'And may God . . . grant that you may agree with one another after the manner of Christ Jesus, and so with one mind and one voice may praise the God and Father of our Lord Jesus Christ' (Rom. 15.5–6) or, 'and every tongue confess that Jesus Christ is Lord, to the glory of God the Father (Phil. 2.11). In Rom. 6.4, although the passage is not doxological in the way that Rom. 15 and Phil. 2 are, we still have the statement 'as Christ was raised from the dead through the glory of the Father'.

This evidence means, I suggest, that the recognition of God as Father is something which happens on the far side of the transforming experience Paul describes in the language of dying and rising. Discovering God as Father is the experience of those, and only those, who are sons (and daughters): 'To prove that you are sons, God has sent into our hearts the

Spirit of his son crying "Abba! Father!"' (Gal. 4.6; cf. Rom. 8.15).

Perhaps the familiarity of Christian tradition, and particularly the over-familiarity of the Lord's Prayer, has obscured the richness of the content of the word 'Father', and the fact that a person cannot say *abba* outside a filial relationship of faith.

So Paul's language about God, and his understanding of God, is profoundly experiential, as we would expect. The new experience of God to which he testifies is appropriated through a person becoming a son/daughter. As always in the New Testament, this is both a present experience and a future hope: 'For those whom God knew before ever they were, he also ordained to share the likeness of his Son, so that he might be the eldest among a large family (of brothers)' (Rom. 8.29).

So it is Jesus' own Sonship which he communicates to us.

There is no hint of degrees of sonship; no suggestion that He keeps for Himself the perfect type and bids us be content with a second best . . . He is the Son, unique and essential, not because He will keep anything back from us which He possesses in His eternal oneness with the Father . . . The uniqueness of His Sonship consists, not in any part of His consciousness and joy or toil that He reserves for Himself, but in the entire fullness of it that He gives.[10]

So divine Sonship has a cruciform pattern; it is the imprint given to it by Jesus, to whom are attributed the words: 'He who has seen me has seen the Father' (John 14.9).

The cross and resurrection, then, are to be understood as the supreme revelation of the Fatherhood of God and the Sonship of Jesus. In that 'he became obedient to death, death on a cross' (Phil. 2.8), the cross was the ultimate demonstration of the Son's trust and obedience. The writer to the

Hebrews put it rather differently: for him the perfection of Christ consists in the completion of his obedience: '. . . although a son, he learned obedience through his sufferings, and having been perfected, he became the cause of eternal salvation for all who obey' (Heb. 5.8–9).

In a quite different way, Matthew's Gospel associates the death of Jesus with his divine Sonship. In what appear to be additions to Mark's account, and in language which echoes the Temptations, the evangelist implies that the cross is *both* the supreme test *and* the revelation of his Sonship: 'Save yourself, if you are the Son of God, and come down from the cross' (27.40 – cf.v.43).

This supreme revelation of the Father and the Son finds explicit expression in John's Gospel: 'Father, the hour has come ; glorify your Son, that the Son may glorify you' (John 17.1). This verse underlines a theme we noted in the previous chapter: the *inseparability* of Father and Son: 'I am in the Father and the Father in me' (John 14.11).

What, then, does the cross or, rather, the cross and resurrection together, say about the Fatherhood of God? In Pauline language the cross expresses the weakness and foolishness of God (I Cor. 1.25): the ultimate act of self-emptying (Phil. 2.5). It is a *kenosis* foreshadowed, in a curious way, in the parable of the prodigal son. This parable portrays no ordinary father, but a father who gave his son the share due to him of his inheritance (*tes ousias*, lit. 'being') (Luke 15.12). And the parable immediately goes on to say the father gave to his sons his 'livelihood' (*bion*, lit. 'life'). So it was the father's own *life and being* which were expended in the far country, as the elder son bitterly complains in v.30.

The letter to the Hebrews points in the same direction, though in very different language, when the writer refers in the opening verses to the Son who is 'the very stamp of his (i.e. God's) being' (Heb. 1.3), and goes on, in one of the rare New Testament instances of this, to address Jesus as God:

but of the Son he says,
'your throne, O God, is for ever and ever,
and the righteous sceptre is the sceptre of your kingdom'
(v.8).

The logic of the ensuing argument of this letter is that *God* is both high priest and sacrifice.

This divine *kenosis* or self-emptying is the meaning of the 'handing over' of the Son by the Father, and of the 'silence' of the *abba* in heaven to whom his Son prayed 'Let this cup pass from me.'

But all of this can be said only because the resurrection is also understood as *the* demonstration of divine power, comparable only with creation itself, as Rom. 4.17 shows, with its reference to 'the God who makes the dead live, and calls into being the things which are not'.

So 'the Father' is perceived clearly *only* through the cross and resurrection. Without that lens, oppressive power, patriarchy and legalistic concepts of justice distort the picture.

To return, finally, to the point from which we began: how did the revelation of the God and Father of Jesus Christ affect the context into which it came? In particular, what of those features in the God-language of Jewish writings of the time, which we noted at the beginning of this chapter?

First, *the language of particularity* has disappeared from Paul's writings. The apostle does not take over the language of the Old Testament undiscriminatingly: expressions such as 'the Holy One of Israel' do not appear at all in Paul. Other expressions, such as 'Lord of hosts' – translated in the Greek Old Testament as *kyrios sabaoth*, or *kyrios pantokrator* – are used only in Old Testament quotations (Rom. 9.29 and II Cor. 6.18). The reason for this is not far to seek: 'Do you suppose God is the God of the Jews alone? Is he not the God of Gentiles also?' (Rom. 3.29) But we need to ask: can this change in language be explained by reference to Christ, and related to the broader context of our inquiry?

The answer lies in what Paul believed about Jesus and the Law. The Law had now become God's *pen*ultimate word to humankind; it could now be seen as an interlude between Abraham and Christ. But what had happened that relativized the Law in this way? The letter to the Ephesians (probably by a later interpreter of Paul) makes explicit what is said more indirectly in the undisputed letters:

> For he himself is our peace. Gentiles and Jews, he has made the two one, and in his own body of flesh and blood has broken down the barrier of enmity which separated them; for he annulled the law with its rules and regulations, so as to create out of the two a single new humanity in himself, thereby making peace. This was his purpose, to reconcile the two in a single body to God through the cross, by which he killed the enmity (2.14–16).

The Greek here is somewhat rambling and repetitious, but *hostility* is identified with the Law: the Law is the (cause of?) the hostility – and the cross removed it. So the Jew-Gentile hostility died with Christ.

Of the undisputed letters of Paul, Galatians comes nearest to 'explaining' what happened in the death of Christ. The Law was given because of human transgressions, says Paul (3.19); it was promulgated by angels at the hand of an intermediary (v.20) presumably Moses. But whilst Moses cannot be said to have been acting for the whole human race (if that is what Paul's very obscure Greek in the first half of v.20 means), Paul's argument traces a *universal* strand in God's dealings with human-kind, beginning with Abraham ('In you all nations shall find blessing', v.8), and culminating in Christ. The number one, as N. T. Wright has pointed out, is crucial to the argument: one seed, namely Christ (v.16), one God (v.20), and one people (v.28).

But it was Christ's *death* which removed 'the curse' of the Law (v.13). It is not clear, from the immediate context of this verse, how this was achieved. The answer lies in the way in which God must now, as it were, be defined: '. . . God the Father *who raised him from the dead*' (1.1).

The significance of where this seminal statement occurs in the letter, at its very beginning, has often been overlooked. It is as if Paul is saying: this new understanding of God under-pins the whole of my ensuing argument. In particular, whilst the Law placed Christ under its curse (3.13) God, through the resurrection, overruled the verdict of the Law, thus creating one people, 'for there is no such thing as Jew or Greek' (3.28a).

A later statement in the letter expresses more fully the 'exchange' outlined in 3.13: '. . . but when the appointed time came, God sent his Son, born of a woman, born under the Law, to buy freedom for those who were under the Law, in order that we might attain the status of sons' (4.4–5).

So new creation, and sonship and justification no longer have anything to do with being a Jew or becoming a Jew. The 'mould' has been broken, so to speak. We can see this in both the prototype and anti-type of Christ in Paul's letters. The prototype is Abraham, accepted by God before ever he became a Jew (Gen. 15.6, quoted in both Gal. 3.6 and Rom. 4.3); the antitype is Adam, who, by definition, is a universal not a national figure.

So the language of particularity applied to God is, for Paul, at an end. Here is one of the clearest examples of discon-tinuity between the old and the new understandings of God.

The second characteristic of the Jewish literature of this period arose from the deepening crisis in Palestine: if God is God of Israel, how can his people, and his land, be oppressed and overrun by Gentiles? But now, because the era of par-ticularity (Rom. 3.29, Gal.3.28 etc.) is over, the nature of the crisis changes. 'The righteousness of God is being revealed'

(Rom. 1.17), even though Roman armies continue to tramp through the land of Israel.

There was a theodicy problem – can God be justified? – and it arose from the dark mystery of the rejection of God's Messiah by most of God's people, Israel. (Paul addresses the issue at length in Rom. 9–11). But one remarkable difference between New Testament perspectives and our own lies in how little attention is paid by New Testament writers to 'the problem of suffering' (as C. S. Lewis called it). Here there is no agonizing struggle to reconcile theology with reality.

The reason for this appears to be twofold. First the resurrection transforms the crucifixion. Or, to put this another way, the cross is the essential context in which and from which God's creative power is revealed. In the same way the sufferings of Paul were to be the means by which 'the life of Jesus' was revealed (II Cor. 4.7–12). Neither the sufferings of Jesus nor the sufferings of Paul are the kind of suffering which people today have in mind when they speak of the 'problem' of suffering. We usually mean the appalling results of natural disasters such as earthquakes, or a child struck down by cancer. *These* theodicy questions, which concern us so much, feature hardly at all in the New Testament. Nevertheless, the cross with its message of a crucified God provided both an icon, and an existential position, which enabled people to live creatively with 'the mystery of suffering' in its many dimensions.

A second reason why New Testament writers seem less anguished than some of their Jewish contemporaries lies in their future perspective arising out of their resurrection faith. Paul expresses this well: 'I realize that the sufferings we now endure bear no comparison with the glory, as yet unrevealed, which is in store for us' (Rom. 8.18).

Of course, this future perspective can be found in Jewish writings, both in the Old Testament, and in later writings.

But hope and despair for the Christian were no longer related to the fate of the land of Israel.

Finally, we look again at the Old Testament and Jewish language of grace, and the relation of Paul's language about God – explicit and implicit – to 'Jesus and his God'.

There was a tendency – evident in some passages in the Targums, and in the Book of Jubilees[11] – to imply that God chose Abraham and Jacob because they had already demonstrated their worthiness. Paul, particularly in Romans and Galatians, counters that, although that should not lead us to inaccurate and unfair generalizations such as 'Judaism believed in salvation by works'. But, more than that, Paul's language now reflects his conviction that God's grace is universal. What Paul seems to have done is to use two different Greek words for the Hebrew *ḥeṣed* – God's covenantal loving kindness: *eleos* is used particularly, but not exclusively, of God's love for Israel – so it appears in Rom. 9–11 more often than in the rest of Paul's writings put together. *Charis*, usually translated 'grace', seems to be used more widely, but especially when Paul is expounding the universal benefits of Christ's work.

It would be a serious mistake to overlook the frequency of the language of grace in the Old Testament and other Jewish literature, but equally we should not overlook the *radical* nature of Paul's language, not least in Rom. 5.12–21. Christ and Adam have this in common: their effect, so to speak, was/is universal. But there the analogy ends, and Paul's tortuous Greek here reflects his attempt both to compare and contrast Adam with Christ. An extraordinary difference is outlined in v.16: whereas condemnation followed the sin of *one* man, an act of grace followed the transgression of *many*. The logic of this seems plain: the more sin, the more grace (v.20),[12] leading to the understandable, but erroneous question: 'Are we to go on sinning, that grace may abound?' (6.1).

So it may be said that Paul both *radicalized and univers-*

alized the language of grace which he inherited through the traditions of Israel. But his Adam language shows that it was precisely by this kind of language, including the language of justification, that he expresses how a human being begins to receive the divine imprint.

To summarize: Paul's language is different in many ways from the language of the Gospels. For example, Kingdom of God language is marginal in Paul; expressions such as 'the Lord Jesus Christ' and 'in Christ' are conversely very prominent. It is not easy to relate the two. The heart of the matter, I suggest, lies in seeing the cross and resurrection as *the* revelation of both the Fatherhood of God and the Sonship of Jesus. That means:

1. The divine imprint on a human life acquires a cruciform pattern, as exemplified in the life of Paul. To put this another way, the experience of God's Fatherhood and of sonship is gained through the dying and rising described in Rom. 6.1–11.

2. The Fatherhood of God, of which Jesus spoke, expresses itself in self-sacrifice and creative power – the two belonging inseparably together.

3. The Kingdom of God now has Jesus-like contours: 'the Lord Jesus Christ' stands for 'Kingdom of God'.

3

When the Image Fades

The first two chapters have drawn attention to the insepar-ability of the Fatherhood of God and the Sonship of Jesus. Many strands of New Testament theology meet at this point, including the portrayal of Jesus as Son of David, with the recurring use of the coronation psalm (Ps. 2), 'You are my son . . . this day I become your father' (v.7b), and the theme of 'the last Adam' and 'new creation', with the motif of the divine image perceived again in Jesus.

Today, however, the biblical concept of the image of God, like much else in our culture, tends to be interpreted individualistically. It is most frequently defined as the 'spiri-tual dimension' of a person, although it is not always clear what that means. In his recent book *Text, Church and World*, Francis Watson, drawing on the work of Alistair McFadyen (*The Call to Personhood*, 1990) points out that the Genesis narratives do not support this individualistic interpretation of God's image in humans. Rather, they offer a 'relational, dialogical understanding'[1] of the image of God. God himself engages humankind in dialogue, rather than haranguing it in monologue, and according to the first creation story, the image of God is closely related to the creation of humankind, not in the form of an isolated indi-vidual, but as male and female: 'God created human beings in his own image, in the image of God he created them; male and female he created them' (Gen. 1.27). There is a similar theme in the second creation story, although not explicitly linked here with the image of God: 'It is not good for the man to be alone' (2.18).

It is not unfanciful, I think, to link this relational under-standing of the divine image in humans, in both aspects, with the answer of Jesus to the question 'Which is the first of all the commandments?' (Mark 12.28b). But our concern here is more directly theological. What does the New Testament have to say about the opposite process to salvation, that is, when the image fades or grows faint? How are we to under-stand the judgment and wrath of God?

It should hardly need saying that the concept of wrath expressed in a newspaper headline the day after York Minster was struck by lightning some years ago is a far cry from much of what the Bible has to say about wrath. Of course, some biblical stories might seem to support that view. But it is important in this, as in most matters, to identify the different kinds of literature, and the different kinds of language, within the Bible. So, for example, the stories of the Flood (Gen. 6–7), and of the Tower of Babel (Gen. 11.1–9) have the character of myth. Like other such stories, the point is not whether they are historically true, but what they are meant to convey. It will be best to start, not from a crudely literalist concept of divine punishments, but a more existenti-alist one, as for example, in Psalm 90:

> We are brought to an end by your anger,
> terrified by your wrath.
> You set our iniquities before you,
> our secret sins in the light of your presence.
> All our days pass under your wrath;
> our years die away like a murmur (vv.7–9).

With this passage from the Psalms may be compared this extract from an essay by a modern theologian:

What is it that is responsible for this passing, that dooms our human faith to frustration? We may call it the nature of things, we may call it fate, we may call it reality. But by whatever name we call it, this law of things, this reality, this way things are, is something with which we all must reckon. We may not be able to give a name to it, calling it only the 'void' out of which everything comes and to which everything returns, though that is also a name. But it is there – the last shadowy and vague reality, the secret of existence by virtue of which things come into being, are what they are, and pass away. Against it there is no defense. This reality, this nature of things, abides when all else passes. It is the source of all things and the end of all. It surrounds our life as the great abyss into which all things plunge and as the great source whence they all come. What it is we do not know save that it is and that it is the supreme reality with which we must reckon.[2]

This, I suggest, can be the starting-point for our exploration of what the Bible means by the wrath of God. It is closely related to a statement about God in the New Testament which may owe much to Stoic influence, but is no less important for all that. It comes in Paul's sermon at Athens: '. . . in him we live and move, in him we exist . . .' (Acts 17.28). But the passage to which we turn first may be said to contain the New Testament's fullest exposition of divine wrath. It is Rom. 1.18–32:

Divine retribution is to be seen at work, falling from heaven on all the impiety and wickedness of men and women who in their wickedness suppress the truth. For all that can be known of God lies plain before their eyes; indeed God himself has disclosed it to them. Ever since the world began his invisible attributes, that is to say his everlasting power and deity, have been visible to the eye of

reason, in the things he has made. Their conduct, therefore, is indefensible; knowing God, they have refused to
honour him as God, or to render him thanks. Hence all
their thinking has ended in futility, and their misguided
minds are plunged in darkness. They boast of their
wisdom, but they have made fools of themselves, exchanging the glory of the immortal God for an image shaped like
mortal man, even for images like birds, beasts, and reptiles.

For this reason God has given them up to their own vile
desires, and the consequent degradation of their bodies.

They have exchanged the truth of God for a lie, and
have offered reverence and worship to created things
instead of to the Creator. Blessed is he for ever, Amen. As
a result God has given them up to shameful passions.
Among them women have exchanged natural intercourse
for unnatural, and men too, giving up natural relations
with women, burn with lust for one another; males behave
indecently with males, and are paid in their own persons
the fitting wage of such perversion.

Thus, because they have not seen fit to acknowledge
God, he has given them up to their own depraved way of
thinking, and this leads them to break all rules of conduct.
They are filled with every kind of wickedness, villainy,
greed, and malice; they are one mass of envy, murder,
rivalry, treachery, and malevolence; gossips and scandal-
mongers; and blasphemers, insolent, arrogant, and boast-
ful; they invent new kinds of vice, they show no respect to
parents, they are without sense or fidelity, without natural
affection or pity. They know well enough the just decree of
God, that those who behave like this deserve to die; yet
they not only do these things themselves but approve such
conduct in others.

First, we must note the parallelism between divine wrath
and divine righteousness. *Both* are being revealed (present

tense). Verse 17 shows that God's righteousness is being revealed *in the gospel*, and though that is not said of God's wrath, the parallel at least suggests that the Gospel makes clearer a process already at work: in the language of John's Gospel, with the advent of the light, the darkness is exposed for what it is.

What, then, is the wrath of God? It is reasonable to look to the Old Testament for Paul's original understanding of wrath, even if we eventually conclude that the gospel has modified that understanding.

In his book *The Prophets*, Abraham Heschel notes that there is an ambiguity about the pathos of anger: 'As long as the anger of God is viewed in the light of the psychology of passions rather than in the light of the theology of pathos, no adequate understanding will be possible.'[3] Heschel goes on to observe that in the Old Testament prophets, God's wrath is not something arbitrary or unpredictable, it is contingent and temporary; it is preceded and followed by compassion, because the secret of God's anger is God's care.[4] (With this assertion we might compare the definition of God's 'almightiness' as God's ability never to lose control of himself.) This view is preferable to C. H. Dodd's famous definition of divine wrath as 'cause and effect in a moral universe', even though that has more than a grain of truth, as we saw in the earlier discussion of the 'measure for measure' sayings of Jesus.

Turning back to the Romans text, we need to observe (as often with Paul) the tightly knit unity of the argument: connecting words at the beginning of vv.19, 20, 21, 24 and 26 show that Paul is describing a sequence of actions with 'built-in consequences' (a 'downward spiral').[5]

The wrath of God, says Paul (v.18) is directed 'against all the impiety and wickedness of men and women who in their wickedness suppress the truth'. The translation 'wickedness' obscures the fact that the Greek word *adikia* denotes the opposite of God's righteousness (*dikaiosyne*), which means God's faithfulness to his own character, or God's saving goodness. Thus the primary sin is to do the very opposite of what God is doing, and not to live by the norms of creation, thereby suppressing the truth. Such behaviour flies in the face of reality, erasing, if that were possible, the divine image in humankind.

This conduct is especially reprehensible because (vv.19–20) God can actually be known through his creation: 'All that can be known of God lies plain before their eyes . . . their conduct therefore is indefensible.'

So far, we have had no explicit links with the theme of the divine image in humankind. This theme is soon to emerge, although the *adikia* of humankind foreshadows it, since the word indicates the wilful transgression of relational norms (human and divine) which God intended.

What the 'vertical' dimension of the image was meant to be is described in v.21: to glorify God (i.e. reflect back God's being), and to give thanks. *That* is the divine human relationship as it was intended to be, but that is precisely what human beings have not done. The consequence is outlined by Paul in the remainder of v.21 and in v.22: 'Hence all their thinking ended in futility, and their misguided minds are plunged in darkness. They boast of their wisdom, but they have made fools of themselves . . .'

The REB translation partly obscures the fact that three of the verbs here are passive, almost certainly indicating divine agency: *God* made futile their reasonings, darkened their minds, and made them foolish. The consequences for humankind are disastrous: if the mind (literally, 'the heart') has been darkened, a person will not even perceive, let alone will, what is good and true. This does not mean that people are aware of, or acknowledge this. That only comes to light with the gospel (cf. I Cor. 1–2). People who lose touch with reality may be the last to realize it.

The foolishness of human beings, as outlined here by Paul, manifests itself in one particular way: they are no longer capable of distinguishing between the Creator and the created. As one commentator puts it: 'All their thinking suffers from the fatal flaw, the basic disconnection from reality involved in their failure to recognize and glorify the true God.'[6] And so 'they exchanged the glory of the immortal God for an image shaped like mortal man, even for images like birds, beasts and reptiles' (v.23).

With this verse we encounter one of two verbs which Paul uses three times each in the succeeding verses. A discussion of these two verbs will help to provide an overview of the ensuing argument, and the theology implied in it, without a full exegesis of each verse.

The first verb is the verb to *exchange*: 'they exchanged the glory of the incorruptible God . . .' (v.23); 'they have exchanged the truth of God for a lie . . .' (v.25), and 'women have exchanged natural intercourse for unnatural, and men, too, giving up natural relations with women, burn with lust for one another' (v.27a).

There is a double meaning in the first occurrence of this verb: as they worshipped idols (human and animal) (Deut. 4.16–17), *so they became like them*. The same theme is to be found in Psalm 115:

Their idols are silver and gold, made by human hands,
They have mouths, but cannot speak,
eyes but cannot see . . .
Their makers become like them,
and so do all who put their trust in them' (vv.4–8).

So Paul is here expressing a biblical conviction that when people worship what is less than God, they become less than human. The divine image begins to fade. This is the first step of the 'downward spiral': idolatry leads to dehumanization. (Eberhard Jüngel, a leading Lutheran theologian, stresses the importance of the upright stance of human beings, and so the reference here to four-legged creatures ['things that crawl' 'beasts and reptiles', REB] may be significant.)

But now we turn to the second key verb of this passage. 'God has given them up to their own vile desires' (v.24); 'God has given them up to shameful passions' (v.26); 'God has given them up to their own depraved way of thinking' (v.28). Thus the human response of exchanging God's glory for 'inferior, shadowy substitutes' (C. K. Barrett), reality for unreality, natural for unnatural, is met by a divine response: 'God gave them up . . .' What does this mean?

In v.24 Paul means: 'their own vile desires, and the consequent degradation of their bodies' *was* the prison into which God delivered people. There are similar expressions elsewhere in Paul, using a different, but related verb: '. . . in shutting all mankind in the prison of their disobedience, God's purpose was to show mercy to all mankind' (cf. Gal. 3.22 for this concept of being enclosed by God or by an agent of God). Paul, like Amos, had a powerful sense of the inescapability of God: Amos 9.1b–2 is the negative counterpart to Ps. 139: 'No fugitive will escape, no survivor find safety. Though they dig down to Sheol, from there my hand will take them; though they climb up to the heavens, from there shall I bring them down.'

The God who by his grace calls us into freedom is the same God who in his wrath allows people to experience the consequences of their wrongdoing, and that, not because he is vindictive, but because he is holy and merciful. 'We cannot sin ourselves out of the structures of our being as persons in personal relationship with God, which is the saving factor in our otherwise desperate situation.'[7]

In Rom. 1.24 then, 'uncleanness' was the prison into which God delivered people. Their own desires (*epithumiais*) are the human instrument of that imprisonment, the thought being that human desires are projected on to external phenomena in a disordered and even perverted way. The result is the dishonouring of their own persons (or bodies).

So there are two forces at work in the downward spiral: 1. human *exchange* (better than human choice or freewill) and 2. divine wrath, evidenced in God's 'active consent to the working out of human sin into its inevitable consequences.'[8]

We can now briefly summarize the remainder of this passage. Idolatry, Paul has argued, leads to dehumanization, and the consequent disordering of human life becomes apparent, first, in sexual relationships (vv.24 and 26–27) and, finally, as indicated in the lengthy catalogue of vices in vv.29–31, in social disintegration, because sin has poisoned human relationships, draining them of trust, generosity and mercy.

The theological root of this degeneration is made very clear by the repeated verb 'God gave them up' (vv.26 and 28), but also by word-links not always apparent in translation. There is an example in v.28: '. . . because they have not seen fit (*edokimasan*) to acknowledge God, he has given them up to their own depraved way of thinking . . .' (*eis adokimon noun*); that means, their minds become unfit for anything, least of all moral discernment. Similarly, because people do not honour God (v.21, although the word 'honour' is not used), their sin recoils on them, with the result that they dishonour themselves (v.24).

It is possible that behind these verses lies Paul's understanding of the story of Adam in Genesis. Whether that is so or not, we are given here a picture of creation unravelling in a downward spiral. The divine image fades, as humankind freewheels from idolatry to dehumanization and social disintegration. How this is to be interpreted today is a question to which I shall return. But it is worth raising here the related question of whether we should adopt the theism expressed in this passage. There is a tantalizingly brief discussion in H. J. Cadbury's *The Peril of Modernizing Jesus* of what the author calls the 'unmodern theism' of Jesus. Cadbury contends that Jesus attributed some things to the personal agency of God which modern people would not. Three points may briefly be made. First, however radical the thought may seem, we cannot, if the concept of incarnation is to be taken seriously, exempt Jesus' ideas about God from the cultural-conditioning which is a universal phenomenon in human life. The reality of Jesus' intensely personal experience of and understanding of God is not thereby undermined. Second, we need to be wary of making 'modernity' the criterion by which all things are evaluated; what is 'modern' is as culturally conditioned and relative as everything else. We moderns may have 'blind spots' which people of biblical times did not have. Thirdly, our understanding of God cannot be a purely cerebral matter; it is also a profoundly experiential one. Our own religious experience will shape our answers to the kind of question raised in Cadbury's book.

I have spent some time on this passage because it is the most extended, and perhaps the most profound, exposition of what a major New Testament writer means by the wrath of God. But now we must widen our scope to try to understand more fully this concept of wrath, and the related theme of divine judgment.

It seems natural to consider first other references in Paul's writings to wrath. It would be tedious to discuss them all, but some observations may be made, along with a consideration of how Paul reconciled his understanding of divine wrath with divine love.

Wrath, like righteousness, salvation and other words, has a present and a future dimension in Paul's thought. (For a reference to future wrath, see I Thess. 1.10.) Whether Paul understood future wrath as final (i.e. irreversible) is not easy to determine. I Thess. 2.14–16 is notoriously difficult:

You, my friends, have followed the example of the

Christians in the churches of God in Judaea: you have been treated by your own countrymen as they were treated by the Jews, who killed the Lord Jesus and the prophets and drove us out, and are so heedless of God's will and such enemies of their fellow men that they hinder us from telling the Gentiles how they may be saved. All this time they have been making up the full measure of their guilt. But now retribution has overtaken them for good and all!'

That final phrase (v.16b) may be translated 'wrath has overtaken them *until the end*. If the REB translation 'for good and all' is retained it may be asked how Paul's thought here is to be reconciled with Rom. 11.25–32, which expresses the conviction that in the end 'all Israel' will be saved. Even if we set aside this difficult text, other references to future wrath such as Romans 5.9 (lit. 'we shall be saved through him from wrath') do not make clear whether that wrath is final and irreversible.

Abraham Heschel stresses the transient character of God's wrath in the Old Testament, devoting a separate chapter to the *Ira Dei* ('Wrath of God') and what he understandably (as a Jewish scholar) considers the baleful distortion of the Old Testament by Marcion and all his subsequent followers.[9] But if Heschel is correct in his understanding of the Old Testament, Paul's understanding in Rom. 2.5 seems to be that of an ultimate and final wrath : 'In the obstinate impenitence of your heart you are laying up for yourself a store of retribution (lit. "wrath") against the day of retribution, when God's just judgment will be revealed.'

It is important to define God's wrath in the light of the testimony of both the Old and New Testaments to his love. Two features of the biblical testimony to God need to be affirmed. First, as we noted earlier, God is not simply *a* being, detached from, or separate from, his creation. Rather God is the reality – the *transcendent* personal reality – in whom we

exist. Second, God is not schizophrenic, unpredictable or
arbitrary in his character or actions. So it follows from these
two fundamental convictions, as John Robinson has argued,
that 'There is resolute refusal throughout the Bible to allow
that any person or thing can fall out of this personal relationship to God . . . The New Testament insists on preserving the
recognition that even the most iron laws of cause and effect,
physical and moral, represent in the last analysis the opera-
tion of the divine love.'[10]

Perhaps we should conclude that here is one of the important imprecisions of scripture, or what we might call one of its
creative ambiguities, or even contradictions. There is no easy-
going universalism, but there is also no premature abandonment of anyone, not even the Pharisees of Matthew's Gospel,
the Pharaoh and unbelieving Israel of Rom. 9–11, or 'the
kings of the earth' of the Book of Revelation. For example,
Matt. 23, despite its searing criticisms of the Pharisees, may
(although this is not certain) strike a note of hope even for
them in the concluding verse (39): 'I tell you, you will not see
me until the time when you say "Blessed is he who comes in
the name of the Lord!"'

As for 'the kings of the earth' of Revelation, who in earlier
chapters of the book have been enemies of God, they finally
(21.24) bring 'their glory' into the heavenly Jerusalem itself.

With reference to present wrath, it may be asked whether
such wrath is hidden or revealed. According to Rom.
1.18–32, it is revealed but, like the mystery of the cross in I
Cor. 1–2, it is revealed to those with eyes to see. It is by no
means obvious. But how is such a reality, hidden and
revealed, to be understood?

It is more accurate to speak in this context of the hiddenness of God, rather than the absence of God. The hiddenness
of God is a prominent theme in the Old Testament, integral
rather than peripheral to Israel's faith, and integral, too, to
God's character. A recent study of this theme refers to an

adaptation in Old Testament literature of the hiddenness motif which is 'virtually unparalleled in Near Eastern literature . . . an experience of Yahweh's hiddenness which was peculiarly Israel's painful possession.'[11]

God's hiddenness is not always the result of his wrath, but sometimes that *is* so, especially in the prophets, as in Isa. 64:

When you showed your anger, we sinned
and in spite of it, we have done evil from of old.
We all became like something unclean . . .
There is none who invokes you by name
or rouses himself to hold fast to you;
for you have hidden your face from us
and left us in the grip of our iniquities (vv.5, 6a, 7).

In the Old Testament, the 'face' of God is the source of light ('Lift up the light of your countenance upon us', Num. 6.25), and so when God turns his face away from his people, they are plunged into darkness. Except in quotations from the Greek Old Testament, Paul avoids anthropomorphisms such as 'hand' or 'face', but it is noteworthy that in contexts where he is expounding, explicitly or implicitly, the consequences of divine wrath, he uses the image of darkness: '. . . knowing God, they have refused to honour him as God, or to render him thanks. Hence all their thinking is ended in futility, and their misguided minds are plunged in darkness' (Rom. 1.21) and 'May their eyes become darkened and blind! Bow down their backs unceasingly!' (Rom. 11.10, quoting Ps. 69.23; cf. 11.8).

With this motif of light and darkness in mind, we turn next to the Gospel of John in order to explore further the themes of divine wrath and judgment.

There is much to be said for starting where John starts, namely the prologue: the reader is informed from the start where life, and so presumably truth and reality, are to be found:

In the beginning the Word already was, the Word was in
God's presence, and what God was, the Word was . . . In
him was life, and that life was the light of mankind'
(1.1,4).

The evangelist goes on to say two more things about the light
in the prologue: 'The light shines in the darkness, and the
darkness has never mastered it' (v.5), and then, after emphasizing that John the Baptist was not the light, but was a
witness to it, he goes on:

'The true light which sheds its light on everyone was even
then coming into the world. He was in the world, the
world was made by him, and the world did not recognize
him' (vv.9–10) .

(I have translated the Greek word *photizei*) as 'sheds its
light on', rather than 'enlightens' as this fits better with this
Gospel's theology of judgment: the coming of the light either
draws people to the light – and so to life – or it drives them
(further?) into the darkness, and so to judgment. (See the
reference to 3.19–21below).

Here, in fact, is the foundation of what this Gospel has
to say about judgment. The themes of the prologue are
developed in the Gospel which follows in a remarkable way.
Three features relevant to our theme stand out:

1. The Gospel is full of forensic language, the language
of witnessing, prosecuting, judging. It may reflect the self-
understanding of the Johannine community: they felt themselves to be on trial in an uncomprehending, hostile world.

2. This Gospel is more apocalyptic than first meets the eye.
A central feature of apocalyptic writing is the way in which
it portrays the basic unity and structural parallelism of the
earthly and heavenly realms. That is what we have in John:
the judgment revealed or made on earth is one with the judgment made in heaven.

3. But that is not how it looks to most people. 'He was in the world . . . and the world did not recognize him.' Alongside this fundamental unity of the earthly and heavenly realms, there is also conflict and ignorance. This is the basis of the pervasive irony of this Gospel. Irony in John works as irony because the whole 'drama' operates on two levels, between which there is conflict, and the 'lower level' ('the world') just does not perceive how things really are: 'He was in the world; but the world, though it owed its being to him, did not recognize him. He came to his own, and his own people would not accept him' (1.10–11).

This, then, is the context: a world of conflicting truth claims, in which decisions for and against the truth, and consequently divine judgment, both hidden and revealed, occur.

In view of the prologue, this Gospel's definition of judgment in chapter 3 should come as no surprise. Language about 'the Word' has been replaced by the language about the sending of the Son (3.16). The Son's mission is not to judge (i.e. condemn) the world but to save it (v.17), and the person who believes in the Son is not being condemned, but the one who has not so believed is condemned already (v.18). And then the definition: 'This is the judgment (*krisis*), the light has come into the world, but people preferred darkness to light because their deeds were evil' (v.19). The consequence of this preference is made clear, implicitly in the prologue, explicitly here: it is death, because this light is 'life' (v.4). So the coming of Jesus is the origin of the judgment. Rudolf Bultmann is worth quoting at length on 3.17–21:

In this event (i.e. the mission of the Son) the judgment of the world takes place . . . Moreover, if this event is grounded in the love of God, it follows that God's love is the origin of the judgment . . . Unbelief, by shutting the door on God's love, turns his love into judgment. For this is the meaning of judgment, that man shuts himself off

from God's love . . . with the mission of the Son, this judgment has become a present reality.[12]

(Perhaps a comparison is to be made here between the
simultaneous or parallel revelations in Romans 1 of God's
righteousness and his wrath).

Before we leave John 3, we note the only occurrence of
'wrath' in this gospel: 'Whoever disobeys the Son will not see
that life; God's wrath rests upon him.' This predicament, of
God's wrath 'resting' on someone, is the very opposite to the
status of the Son, of whom it has been said (1.32), the Spirit
of God descended and rested on him. So wrath is to be understood here, not simply as disapproval, but as the way in
which God is experienced: his absence from human life. Yet
it means more than the divine 'absence'; it means God's
exclusion or withdrawal, demonstrated in people's preference of unreality to reality, falsehood to truth (so this
Gospel), in social disintegration, and the impersonalizing and
degradation of human relationships (so Paul), or simply in
the experience of the transience and mortality of all things
human (so Psalm 90, and especially v.9: 'All our days pass
under your wrath; our days die away like a murmur.'

As often in John, a statement made in one passage is re-
stated in another in a slightly different way, and developed at
greater depth. So 5.24 picks up the theme of 3.15 and 3.35:
'Truly, truly, I tell you: the one who hears my word and
believes in the one who sent me has eternal life, and does not
come to judgment, but has passed from death to life.' In John
5 we have a hint of another theme about judgment which is
developed further in subsequent chapters: Jesus' judgment is
just (v.30) – that is, authentic and right. The contrast with
human judgments, which, according to this Gospel, are
usually superficial and therefore wide of the mark, is not
explicitly made here, but it will be later on: 'Stop judging by
appearances; be just in your judgments' (7.24; cf. 8.15–16).

Human judgments tend to be based on appearance, and on criteria which are all too human, but the judgment of Jesus is unerringly true because he is one with the Father (the Word who is God), and so he is the light who illuminates all; in him the truth about human existence is disclosed.

Because human judgments are sometimes badly mistaken, the judgment of God may be surprising and unexpected. The dividing line comes (and that is part of the meaning of the Greek words *krisis*, 'judgment', and *krino*, judge) where we should least expect it. That is illustrated in the conclusion to the healing of the blind man in chapter 9, where Jesus says: 'For judgment I came into this world, so that those who do not see may see, and those who see may become blind' (v.39). This cryptic saying seems to mean: those who think they can see, when they cannot, are not healed: i.e. 'their sin remains'. That is the judgment: to embrace the darkness, and not to realize it is darkness, to say 'We see' and not to realize that the claim is false.

But a climax approaches in the Gospel of John. Most commentators take the view that the Gospel divides into two sections; chapters 1–12, and chapters 13–20, with chapter 12 being a bridge passage, and its concluding verses (vv.44–50) serving as a summary of the main themes expounded in the preceding chapters. Here we need to pay particular attention to v.31: 'Now is the hour of judgment for this world; now shall the prince of this world be driven out.' The reference, as the next verse shows, is to the lifting up of the Son of Man in the crucifixion and resurrection. But why is this the judgment?

It is important to bear in mind the unity of the 'revelation', as this Gospel presents it: 'the Word was made flesh, and we saw his glory . . .' (1.14). Yet the language of the Gospel throughout the early chapters (for example, in the repeated references to 'the hour' of Jesus – e.g. 2.4, 7.30) alerts the reader to the fact that the climax of the revelation is yet to come – and, if that is so, the heart of the 'judgment', too, has yet to be made known.

Two important clues to the message of John are given in chapters 12 and 13. First, Jesus, in response to the request of 'the Greeks' to see him, responds: 'The hour has come for the Son of Man to be glorified (12.23). Almost certainly, this is to be linked with the emphatic 'now' of v.31: 'Now is the hour of judgment for this world; now shall the prince of this world be driven out.'

The second clue comes in the carefully written introduction to chapter 13, fittingly described by one commentator as the headline for the rest of the Gospel:

> It was before the Passover festival, and Jesus knew that his hour had come and that he must leave this world and go to the Father. He had always loved his own who were in the world, and he loved them to the end' (v.1).

There is an important, and, I think, intentional word-link here with the climax of the passion narrative in chapter 19. In 13.1 the phrase 'to the end' ('he loved them to the end') translates the expression *'eis telos'*. The final word of Jesus in chapter 19 is: 'It is finished (*tetelestai*).' The precise meaning of *eis telos* in 13.1 may be debated, but the phrase must at least mean that Jesus' love survived, and was not submerged by the crisis now unfolding.

But can we be more precise about the *telos*? Sonship in the Bible, as we have observed, denotes origin, character and destiny. In this Gospel all three themes are prominent. The way in which John depicts the crucifixion and the resurrection means that the Father-Son partnership, as it were, remains unbroken. Their oneness is undisturbed. The Son returns whence he came. So from two perspectives, we can say that the crucifixion was the furthest point, and the turning-point of the mission of the Son:

1. He loved until the end/fulfilment; he returned to the Father. This is the ultimate disclosure of the Sonship of Jesus and the Fatherhood of God.

2. The passion narrative is a climax in another sense: it marks the climax of the world's hostility to, and rejection of the Word made flesh. In its judgment of the Son, the world itself is judged: hence the emphatic 'now' of 12.32: 'Now is the judgment of this world . . .' The world has finally – at least, finally in its response to the Word made flesh – rejected the light, and, with the light, the source of its own life.

It is instructive to compare and contrast John and Mark at this point. Mark (with Matthew) has Jesus uttering a cry of dereliction from the cross (15.34), and refers to 'darkness over the whole land' (15.33). Is this God turning away his face? At one level the Gospels appear to contradict one another. But perhaps John should be understood here, as elsewhere, as articulating what he believed to be happening at a level deeper than anyone perceived, and even, deeper, it seems, than Jesus himself felt.

There is one further detail to note. In the prologue the evangelist heralded the story of the gospel with the announcement:

'The light shines in the darkness and the darkness has never mastered it' (1.5).

The verb translated here 'has (never) mastered' (*katelaben*) could, and perhaps should, be translated 'did (not) master'. ('Master' is perhaps the best word to use in translation here, since it helps to convey the double meaning of the Greek *katalambano* 'comprehend' and 'overcome'). The verb is an aorist and may refer to a particular occasion when the darkness did not master the light. If that is so, to which occasion is the evangelist referring? Given the reference to 'in the beginning' in v.1, a likely answer is 'at creation'. But since this author is very fond of words and expressions capable of expressing more than one meaning, it is quite possible that v.5 refers also to the crucifixion, the 'lifting up' or 'glorifying' of the Son of Man: 'The light shines in the darkness, and the darkness did not master it.'

So, in very different imagery, John's Gospel has a theology of judgment and wrath very similar to that of Paul. Grace and judgment, love and wrath belong together; neither can be properly understood without the other. According to Paul, righteousness *and wrath* are being revealed. In John's words, light came into the world, and thereby showed up the darkness for what it is.

Two final points need to be made, the first with reference to the Synoptic Gospels. The command 'Do not judge, and you will not be judged' (Matt. 7.1) cannot mean 'Do not make moral judgments'. There are human actions so depraved that it would be amoral or immoral not to condemn them. The 'measure for measure' saying here is elaborated in the verses that follow with particular reference to not seeing properly (vv.3–5). That is why judgment has to be left to God. God is the only one who *does* see properly: 'God is light, and in him there is no darkness at all' (I John 1.5b). The more judgments we pass in our imperfectly sighted condition, the more our judgments recoil on us. We are back once more to the dictum of Wisd. 11.16: '. . . the instruments of someone's sin are the instruments of his punishment'.

Two parables relate the theme of human judgments to the Gospel itself or, in the terms of the parables themselves, to an employer's and a father's generosity. The generous employer of 20.1–16 (*not* the way to run a business, but perhaps the way to run a family), faced by the angry protests of those who, in their own estimation had borne the burden and heat of the day, asks them 'Why be jealous because I am generous?' (lit. 'is your eye evil because I am good?')

In the other parable, another character makes a similar kind of protest: 'You know how I have slaved for you all these years . . .' (Luke 15.29). Perhaps the theological clue to

both parables lies in Luther's 'As you believe him, so you
have him', or in words about reciprocity in a book called *The
Theology of Jesus* by a scholar of an earlier generation:

> What a man is affects what God can be to him . . . What a
> man is or tries to be to his fellows, conditions what God is
> to him . . . To be judged of God is to be in a position where
> his goodness does not bring us increase of life.[13]

The second point from the Synoptic Gospels applies to all
the New Testament writings: it is important not to overlook
a fundamental tenet of both Jewish and Christian belief in
God: 'Hear, O Israel, the Lord your God is one' (Deut. 6.4).
Applied to the theme of judgment, this means that the
revelation of God's wrath must not be understood apart from
the revelation of God's righteousness. Similarly, the future
coming of the Son of Man cannot be properly understood
apart from his coming in humility and suffering.

We need to hold together theology and anthropology. This
is what the Bible invites us to do, with its claim that humankind is made in the image of God. So the mystery of God,
according to the Bible, is the clue to human existence: the
revelation of the Father and the Son reveals the truth not only
about God, but also the truth about our own existence. That
is the basis of the judgment. This is why the language of
wrath conveys a picture of a world losing its God-given
shape; the image fades, creation starts to unravel. We do not
need to look far to see how much chaos, destruction and
suffering human beings are capable of unleashing on one
another to appreciate why biblical language is often so lurid
and urgent.

Divine judgment then means: the truth of our existence is
God-given: it cannot be invented, or revised, or ignored with
impunity. As Paul at Athens says of the reality of God (the
ens realissimum): 'In him we live and move and have our

being' (Acts 17.28). The Gospel means that *love* is the judgment, because love is the reality, the truth in which we live and move and have our being.

Finally, there is the question of interpretation. The biblical concept of 'wrath' in particular causes difficulties for many people today, and so I end this chapter with some brief reflections on this theme, and two extensive quotations from a theologian who, in my view, has engaged very effectively with this particular interpretative task. It must be acknowledged at once that Paul's perspectives on the Gentile world of his day should not necessarily be transferred or applied directly to the modern, or post-modern world. Nevertheless, an interpreter who stands within the Christian tradition, and for whom the biblical documents are in some way normative, or classical, will attempt to relate the texts with her/his own perceptions, experience, and tradition.

Romans 1.18–32 describe the 'revelation' of God's wrath. It is revealed in what we have called a 'downward spiral': idolatry leads to dehumanization, and dehumanization leads to social disintegration.

We may begin with idolatry. It is easily externalized, and dismissed as a concept irrelevant in modern secular societies. If, however, we bear in mind what idols, according to the Bible, do to people, the picture is very different. Idolatry 'involves the misplacement of hope and trust', and that because idols are contingent things, not absolutes, and as such they 'cannot give life, but only receive it'.[14] So idolatry occurs, one might say, in proportion to the extent that people by virtue of their hoping, trusting and commitments make ultimates out of penultimate things.

The Bible claims there is only one ultimate, namely God. 'Wrath', therefore, is a biblical concept which helps to interpret the dire results of displacing the ultimate by contingent, penultimate things.

As for dehumanization and social disintegration, Wolfhart

Pannenberg has attempted to relate what the Bible says about divine wrath and judgment to our situation in contemporary Europe.

> Our cultural world, it seems, is in acute danger of dying because of the absence of God, if human persons continue to seek in vain for meaning in their personal lives, if increasing numbers fail to develop a sense of their personal identity, if the flood of neurosis continues to rise, if more and more people take refuge in suicide or violence, and if the state continues to lose its legitimacy in the consciousness of its citizens, while the cultural tradition functions according to the rules of supply at the discretion of individual demand, all these are the consequences of the absence of God. But far from indicating the death of God, they suggest, rather, that God is not neglected with impunity.[15]

It may be better to speak here of God's hiddenness, rather than his absence. But Pannenberg is broadly correct, going on to relate this assessment of the contemporary situation both to what Paul says in Romans 1, and to the Old Testament concept of God hiding his face. Pannenberg concludes his discussion:

> The darkness of the absence of God is most dense where it is not even perceived. Contemporary literature and art describe its consequences: the loss of a personal expression in the faces of people and the decomposition of human lives deprived of personal identity; the breakup of human communication and of erotic relations, resulting in loneliness and eruptions of that loneliness in assaults of excessive pity for oneself, in terror against others, and finally in suicide. Even the absence of God as such becomes an issue here and there, the feeling of an 'empty transcendence' . . .

But wherever persons discover the absence of God in the midst of their sufferings, and at the same time (this seems to happen more rarely) wherever they recognize God's absence as evidence of divine judgment and as a consequence of their own behaviour, there God is no longer completely absent, there his presence makes itself felt again. And God's presence to the one who seeks his presence means recovery.[16]

4

The Question of God

The question of God was not a question for people in the ancient world in the way that it is for many people today. Even the Epicureans, who have been described, rightly enough, as atheists in practice, ascribed to the gods a certain kind of existence untouched by and unconcerned with the affairs of the world. It is true that the early Christians were accused of atheism, but, as the second-century apologist Justin Martyr argued (*Apology* I 5–6), not only was the charge false, but the gods whom the Christians refused to acknowledge as gods were, in fact, demons.

The issue for many people in the ancient world was not so much whether God or the gods existed, but whether they did anything (according to Cicero, the Roman politician and man of letters, that was *the* theological question of his day), whether, or in what ways, they were accessible to human beings, and whether, as the magical papyri show, their power could be tapped to enable you to survive in a universe perceived as 'red in tooth and claw'.

It is impossible, but also unnecessary, to generalize about religion in the early Roman Empire. Pagan religion in the Graeco-Roman world was an immensely varied, and in some respects lively affair. Its manifestations ranged from popular magical incantations, through the 'many gods and lords' (I Cor. 8.6), from whose cults one might choose, to the more rarefied philosophies of the upper classes who, like Cicero, were well aware of religion's social usefulness. In at least some of these philosophies, as reflected in the literature of the educated and well-to-do, terminology alternates bewilderingly between the singular 'god' and the plural 'gods' and, in Stoic writers, between 'god' and 'nature', as if the two words denoted the same thing.

In the New Testament we get only tantalizing glimpses of these things: the religious 'underworld' of magic, the rich and varied polytheism, and the more philosophical stances of the educated. But glimpses there are, especially in Acts, and notably in the vivid, though somewhat stylized scene in Athens in Acts 17.

From our knowledge, on the one hand, of New Testament theology and, on the other, of Graeco-Roman religion, we can take this encounter to be typical of many Christian/pagan encounters (and not unlike the already well-established tradition of Hellenistic Jewish apologetics). Only a passing reference to Paul's sermon is possible here, but we note his opening gambit:

Men of Athens, I see that in everything that concerns religion you are uncommonly scrupulous [NRSV: . . . how extremely religious you are in every way]. As I was going round looking at the objects of your worship, I noticed among other things an altar bearing the inscription 'To an unknown God'. What you worship but do not know – this is what I now proclaim' (vv. 22–23).

Archaeology has not verified this precise inscription. But at this time a cult devoted to 'all the gods' was growing in popularity. (The religious equivalent of a comprehensive insurance policy?) So we may be confident that Luke is broadly correct in the picture he draws here.

The speech itself stands in the tradition of Jewish apologetics, in which, as the Letter of Aristeas, written in probably the third century BC, shows, the apologist attempts to establish as much common ground as possible with his audience. (Compare Paul's 'a Jew to Jews . . .' I Cor. 9.20.) A modern Christian writer stands in this same tradition when he writes: 'The widespread ineffectiveness of organized religion today is due to its failure to speak to the pre-religious God-awareness.'[1]

One final point before we leave this wider Graeco-Roman background: New Testament language about God is in one sense extraordinarily limited. The expression which is used far and away more frequently than any other is simply *ho theos*: God. The definite article *ho* is necessary in Greek, otherwise we should have to translate *theos* as '*a* god'. *Ho theos* is the only God there is, the all-encompassing, all-defining mystery in which we live and move (Acts 17.28). This theism offers no basis, as Paul Tillich kept emphasizing, for thinking of God as *a* being, alongside other beings; God is Being-itself, ugly and limited though this expression may be.

To summarize this introductory survey to our theme, there *were* questions about God to be addressed, even though not identical with the questions of our modern society, even though the existence of God (or the gods) was hardly an issue.

In Britain, opinion polls continue stubbornly to record that most people believe in God, although it is quite difficult to be sure what that means for many. It may be a legacy of childhood, or even a wistful hope, but such a belief, however vague or general, indicates a response to life which is at least partly religious.

When we turn to the Jewish world into which Jesus was born, the situation, of course, is very different. The fundamental creed around which all Jews united was 'the Lord our God is One . . .' (Deut. 6.4–8). So whilst monotheism is a more complex, and even diverse phenomenon than is often realized, we naturally describe Judaism as monotheistic.

Here the theological continuity between Jews and Christians (the two groups overlapping for many decades) was much greater than that between pagans and Christians. The important differences derived from what they believed had happened; Jewish Christians, unlike the majority of their compatriots, believed that Jesus Christ fulfilled Israel's hopes and destiny, and to these we now turn.

Jewish eschatological hopes varied a great deal. The hope for a Messiah was only part of a much wider complex of hopes and expectations, and even messianic hopes varied, from the Qumran belief in a royal messiah and a priestly Messiah (if that is the correct interpretation of the Dead Sea Scrolls), to an explicitly Davidic Messiah in the Psalms of Solomon. Although the hopes varied, many were fuelled by the perception of a growing contradiction between the covenantal tradition of a chosen people, with its corollary of a promised land, and the deepening political and economic crisis in Palestine.

So the Christian answer to the question of God, whilst affirming that the God and Father of our Lord Jesus Christ is the God of Abraham, Isaac and Jacob begins, in part at least, from *eschatology* and *christology*. This implies a two-fold conviction: the ultimate (the last days) has dawned, and the Messiah has come. But to say that it begins from eschatology and christology is to say, in effect, that the starting point is the resurrection. It is noteworthy how, in Paul's writings, relative clauses referring to the resurrection ('who raised him from the dead . . .' e.g. Gal. 1.1) function in the New Testament rather like 'who brought you up out of the land of Egypt' functions in the Old Testament: i.e. it is fundamental and definitive.

To make the resurrection the starting-point or, more precisely, the main reference-point, does not mean marginalizing all that preceded it. The resurrection casts an illuminating, confirming light over the teaching, the ministry and, above all, the death of Jesus. This is a crucial point if we are to see clearly what the New Testament is saying about God.

With this in mind, we need to draw out the theological implications of the life and teaching of Jesus. Through his life and teaching, the symbol of God's Kingdom and the metaphor of God's fatherhood received new content and focus. (We need to affirm *both* content *and* focus because what Jesus said and what he did complemented each other.) The cross and resurrection do not annul or contradict this new content and focus, but confirm and universalize them. Thus the concept of God's kingship – that is, how God rules and exercises divine power cannot be understood apart from Jesus, his cross and resurrection. Supporting evidence for this view can be seen in the almost total absence from the New Testament of two Greek words which were used often enough to refer to God or a god in other contexts: *basileus*, 'king', and *despotes*, 'lord'. The word *basileus* occurs only five times as a word for 'God' in the New Testament; its contemporary connotations, particularly perhaps its imperial connotations, may have made it virtually unusable as a term referring to the Kingdom of God revealed by Jesus. And whilst *despotes* should not be translated as 'despot', this word also may have been too associated with oppressive power to be an acceptable word for God.

Just as Jesus is the interpreter of the Kingdom, so the Fatherhood of God cannot be properly understood without its counterpart, the Sonship of Jesus. This means that we must ask, not simply what Jesus *said* about the Fatherhood of God. (In the Synoptic Gospels, as we have seen, that was not very much, although passages such as Matt. 11.25-7, Luke 15.11-32 and Matt. 5.43-8 are immensely important. See the earlier discussion in chapter 1). In addition to what Jesus said, we need to consider what he *did* (on the reasonable assumption that his words and deeds cohered), and what he *was* (on the principle 'Like father, like son'). And, lastly on this subject we need to recall that neither the Fatherhood of God nor the Sonship of Jesus can be fully understood apart from the cross and resurrection: the ultimate goal of the Son's mission, and the ultimate act of self-emptying and creativity by the Father.

But, whilst it is necessary to relate the life and teaching of Jesus, and especially his message of God's Kingdom and Fatherhood, to the cross and resurrection, we also need to engage in the reverse process, and ask: what meaning is given to the cross and resurrection by the life which preceded them?

The death of Christ is often separated in Christian thought and theology from what preceded and followed it. The New Testament does not do that. In all four Gospels, that death is the climax and summary statement of the life of Jesus: the life gives meaning to the death.

Jesus was crucified because of his persistence in his mission to Israel that is, his adherence to his understanding of God's Kingdom and Fatherhood. Similarly, in Paul and all the epistles of the New Testament which treat the subject, the resurrection or exaltation of Jesus (the two terms are often interchangeable) gives meaning to that death.

So in both what preceded and followed the cross, the fundamental question is the question of God. God's kingship and Fatherhood constituted the reality on which the life of Jesus was centred. We may say that he and his followers were deluded, but there is no mistaking the theistic emphasis of the New Testament. And the resurrection is, according to the New Testament, *the* demonstration of God's creative power which, in turn, acquires its meaning from what preceded it.

What are the implications of all this? The revelation is encapsulated in the simple Greek phrase particularly common in Paul: *hyper hemon*, 'for us'.

This 'for us' is presented in the Gospels in various ways. (And here I shall try to confine myself to hard historical evidence.) First, Jesus' prophetic sense of mission to his own people, leading him eventually to Jerusalem, is well documented. His choice of twelve disciples seems to be connected with this. In short, he lived for the reformation and renewal of Israel. Second, the miracles of Jesus, even if we deduct the wrongly-named 'nature-miracles'[2] are one of the best-attested facts of his life. One might say, he lived for the sick. Third, his teaching about the Kingdom of God, and about the Messiahship which he would not claim for himself, and yet at the same time transformed (e.g. Luke 7.22–23), suggests that he lived for God and for the poor:

Go and tell John what you have seen and heard: the blind regain their sight, the lame walk, lepers are made clean, the deaf hear, the dead are raised to life, the poor are brought good news – and happy is he who does not find me an obstacle to faith' (Luke 7.22–23).

Similarly, his association with the 'untouchables', such as tax-collectors and lepers, portray someone who lived for the marginalized.

Of course, this is a bald and somewhat schematized summary. Yet, even if we leave aside, because of insufficient evidence, the claim which used to be made, that Jesus identified himself with the suffering servant of Isaiah 53, there is much to be said for the view that Jesus practised what he preached in loving his neighbour. 'The man for others' is historically well attested.

What did the death and resurrection of Jesus add to this? The answer seems to be that they *radicalized and universalized what was already there*, so much so that Paul could confine his references to Jesus almost entirely to the cross and resurrection, because they encapsulated everything about Jesus which had gone before.

The experience of both Peter and Paul is important here,

Peter because of his failure of nerve and consequent apostasy, and Paul because of his dehumanizing religious zeal. Peter is saved from despair, Paul from destructive zeal, and both, it seems, by an encounter with the risen Christ. There is a question here, of course, about whether we are dealing with hard historical evidence, but the *claim* that both apostles saw the risen Christ is well attested, and the claim, if true, would certainly help to explain what they subsequently did. So *if* Jesus rose from the dead, and appeared to these two apostles, it is not difficult to see why, for both men, this was an overwhelming experience of undeserved divine favour or grace. For both men their encounter with the risen Christ was essentially an experience of forgiveness, since both the religious zeal of his opponents and the cowardice of his disciples had contributed to Jesus' death. The 'for us' became part of their experience: he lived and died *for us*.

So grace is *radicalized* . To 'call' people is, according to the Bible, one of God's defining, primary activities.[3] The call comes irrespective of character and achievements (Abraham, for Paul, was the classic instance.) But now the call still comes, wherever a person is, and however far people have fallen. The experience of Peter and of Paul, if true, illustrated the statement of Paul in Rom. 5.20: '. . . where sin was multiplied, grace immeasurably exceeded it . . .'

Second, grace is *universalized*. The argument of the letter to the Galatians is: God vindicated by raising from the dead one who died accursed by the Law of Moses. Therefore living under the Law is no longer a defining characteristic of a son of God. That national limitation no longer exists.

This universalizing of the mission of the Son of God is clear in all the major New Testament writers. Even if Jesus *did* say 'I was sent only to the lost sheep of the house of Israel' (Matt. 15.24), even if he believed he was dying a martyr's death for the sins of Israel, his followers soon saw things differently. In Paul it is expressed quite simply as 'one man died for all' (II

Cor. 5.14), whilst in the writings of 'John' the writer of the first epistle affirms that Christ was a sacrifice not only for the sins of those who came to believe in him, but for 'the sins of the whole world' (I John 2.2).

This radicalizing and universalizing is true if, and only if, *'God was in Christ'* . The presence of the Creator in the cross and resurrection radicalizes and universalizes the 'for us' which was there in the life and ministry of Jesus. And so the revelation of God, according to the New Testament, can be summarized as 'God for us', which, indeed, is what Paul does:

> God commends his own love towards us, because whilst we were still sinners, Christ died for us (Rom. 5.8).

> If God is for us, who (can be) against us? (Rom. 8.31).

(It follows that elaborate theories of sacrifice and atonement are not required if the death of Christ is interpreted, as it should be, in the light of the life which preceded it, and the resurrection which followed it.)

What was at stake in the crucifixion and resurrection was the *truth* of the Father-Son relationship – that is, its credibility and ultimacy. And that, in turn, raises fundamental questions about the very nature of life and human existence. What is the nature of ultimate reality? Is it somehow personal? Is the universe to be understood in terms of relatedness? Or did life begin with a monologue, and will it end in silence?

Here the protology, as well as the eschatology, of the New Testament is important. In John 17 the Son is portrayed as referring, in prayer to his Father, to 'the glory which I had with you before the world was', and the hymn in Col. 1.15–20 refers to the Son in whom everything in heaven and on earth was created . . . the whole universe has been created through him and for him. He exists before all things, and all things are held together in him (1.16a, c, 17).

So the Father-Son relationship is both primordial and ultimate. It frames the world. If so, the heart of the New Testament revelation is the mystery of the incarnation, or whatever word we use to summarize the conviction 'God sent his Son' and, most central of all, the mystery of the cross and the resurrection.

(The word 'mystery' can be a fig-leaf to hide the nakedness of woolly thinking, yet once language about God has been introduced, it is difficult to avoid it. It is a concept which sits uneasily in our culture, but it helps to safeguard the insight that there is more to life than meets the eye.)

Here, I suggest, we shall understand more fully the mystery of the cross if we take seriously the different perspectives of the Gospels: on the one hand, the Son of God's cry of dereliction: '. . . my God, my God, why have you forsaken me?' (Mark 15.34 and Matt. 27.46). And, on the other hand, his prayer of trust: 'Father, into your hands I commit my spirit' (Luke 23.46), and his cry of victory: 'It is accomplished!' (John 19.30).

The issue is whether the personal relatedness, which finds its deepest and richest fulfilment in love, is the last word in life and the universe, that is, a reality beyond which you cannot go. Behind the early Christian conviction 'God raised Jesus' lies the belief that that indeed is so. the Father-Son relationship was tested to destruction, and held, against suffering, rejection, evil and death.

So far, I may have given the impression that New Testament theology is binitarian. But whilst it is important to hear New Testament writers in their own terms, rather than to read later doctrines into them, there is in the New

Testament a great deal of 'Spirit' language which at least anticipates the later doctrine of the Trinity. In particular, we note II Cor. 13.13: 'The grace of the Lord Jesus Christ, the love of God, and the fellowship of the Holy Spirit be with you all.'

The four evangelists assume – indeed, they explicitly *say* that the Spirit of God is the mode of God's presence in the prophets or in all creation. That is not stated repeatedly in the Gospel narratives: the story of Jesus' baptism expresses what was foundational for his ministry, John making explicit, as often, what was implicit in the others, that 'the Spirit descended and *remained* on him' (1.23). That is why, in the last discourses in the same Gospel, Jesus can refer to the 'Spirit of truth' whom the disciples already know because 'he remains beside them' (i.e. in the person of Jesus) 'and will be in them' (i.e. when Jesus returns to the Father' (14.17).

Once again, we must ask: what takes place in and through the cross and resurrection? One of the several images used is that of 'new creation': just as the return from exile was likened by Deutero-Isaiah to a new Exodus (e.g. Isa. 43.16–19), so now the resurrection and a new community are described as a new creation. In Pauline language, the divine kenosis – that is, God's assumption of weakness and suffering – becomes the locus of divine power through which the life of God, focussed and exemplified in Jesus, now finds expression in others.

The writings of the New Testament are impressively unanimous about the new spiritual possibilities and power which are realized after the resurrection. According to Paul, believers now have 'access' to God through Jesus:

> Therefore, now that we have been justified through faith, we are at peace with God through our Lord Jesus Christ, who has given us access to that grace in which we now live . . . (Rom. 5.1, 2a).

The sonship which was Jesus' can be replicated through the Spirit in the lives of others:

> To prove that you are sons, God has sent into our hearts the Spirit of his Son, crying 'Abba! Father!' you are therefore no longer a slave but a son and if a son, an heir by God's own act (Gal. 4.6–7).

According to Hebrews, Christians now may enter the 'heavenly sanctuary' to which Christ preceded them, and where he now makes intercession on their behalf. According to John, the promised Spirit can only come when the Son has returned to the Father; that is the moment Jesus can refer to God not only as 'my Father' and 'my God', but '*your* Father and *your* God (20.17). This means that the fundamental categories in which the Spirit may be described are christological, missiological and eschatological: christological because wherever the Spirit is given, there is the imprint of Christ, and the divine image is restored; missiological, because the coming of the Spirit is universal and inclusive, and eschatological because the Spirit anticipates the consummation of all things.

So the divine *koinonia* has, according to the New Testament, been extended to embrace potentially everyone. The revelation is the revelation of God – for us. This was evidenced, as we saw, in the coming of God's Kingdom, and its invitation to, and gift of, life – life with and for God. The kingdom revealed was not an oppressive, excluding reality, but a healing, embracing one. It was also evidenced in the way Paul used the phrase 'the righteousness of God'. That does not refer to God's justice, as if it were a moral standard which God sets, but to a *mission:* the righteousness of God is being revealed *in the gospel* (Rom. 1.17), and, as II Cor. 5.21 makes clear, God through Christ gathers other people up into his mission to save the world. In a word, God's righteousness, like his Kingdom, is not something he keeps to himself: he shares it.

With this last point in mind, we turn once more to a Jewish writer whose work has survived in large quantities. Philo is interesting for our study because of the contrast (as well as the similarities) he provides with New Testament writers on the subject of the divine image, and the 'composite' man made up of earthly substance and divine breath (Gen. 2.7). Similarly, in his *Allegorical Interpretation I* he makes the same distinction: there are two types of 'man', one heavenly and one earthly.[4]

In a word, Philo's anthropology, and so his perception of what I am calling the divine imprint on human life, is dominated by dualisms: soul and body, mind and sense-perception, self-mastery and passion or pleasure. For example, the truly religious person, according to Philo, is one who, through self-mastery, has risen above passion and pleasure.

For New Testament writers, there is really only one anthropological dualism, Adam and Christ. Adam represents human beings in their fallenness or, if we adopt the understanding of the Fall first expounded in the second century by Irenaeus, human beings who have not yet attained their God-given potential. Christ represents human beings as God intended them to be: 'the proper Man'. That is a large part of what is meant in the baptism story: 'You are my Son, in you I am well pleased.'

So according to the New Testament, it is Christ who offers the clearest, fullest picture of the divine imprint on a human life. In the first chapter I attempted to show how that imprint was conveyed in the Gospels: the Synoptics represent Jesus as the supreme practitioner of his own teaching about the Kingdom of God, whilst John makes explicit the Father-Son relationship which, I suggested, underlay the other Gospels. In the second chapter we saw, particularly from Paul's self-

descriptions, that that divine imprint has acquired a cruciform pattern: 'dying we live', a life patterned on the crucified
God. Now, in the light of New Testament teaching on the
Holy Spirit, we look at one more pattern of the divine
imprint on human life. The pattern does not contradict the
other two patterns, of Jesus and the Kingdom, and of the
apostle's dying and rising with Christ; it belongs with them,
as a third perspective.

I referred earlier to Paul Tillich's remark 'It takes two to
make a revelation.' He meant that a revelation has to be
received as well as given, otherwise it is not a revelation. In
the New Testament, the word which denotes the human
response to revelation is faith. This is the all-purpose word
which denotes receptivity to the revelation of God in Christ.
Thus faith includes belief, trust and obedience. That it is a distinctively Christian word in the New Testament can be seen,
for example, in Gal. 3.23 with its striking expression 'before
faith came' (cf. the earlier 'until the seed came' in v.19b).

So Paul speaks of the coming of faith. Thus 'faith' is the
gateway to replicating the divine life revealed in Christ in
human life; it is the necessary foundation of the divine
imprint in its fuller, more explicit christological sense. (This
is not to deny Justin Martyr's assertion that Socrates was a
Christian before Christ, nor to deny that Gandhi was Christ-
like without belief in Christ. It is still true that 'faith' is *the*
word denoting receptivity to God's revelation in Christ.)

Once again, an individualistic culture such as ours has
tended to individualize the concept of faith, narrowing and
distorting it. The New Testament shows that response to the
divine revelation in Christ *involves* turning to one's neighbour. Put simply, there is no faith without love. As Paul says
in Gal. 5.6, love is faith's *modus operandi*: faith expresses
itself through love. In view of this, and the centrality in many
contexts in the New Testament of the word 'love', we must
take a little time to explore this overused, devalued word.

Agape had a pre-Christian history in both the Greek Old Testament and in secular Greek, but the gospel invested it with new meaning.[5] The content of the word derives from God. The Greek of I John 4.8 and 16 cannot be translated 'Love is God'. The same writer makes it clear that the death of Christ is the means by which we know what love is: 'This is how we know what love is: Christ gave his life for us . . .' (I John 3.16a).

If the content of this word is determined by God's self-revelation, how will *agape* imprint itself on human life? Two themes stand out clearly. First, there is the movement of *agape* to the other, even when the other is hostile: 'God so loved the world that he gave his only Son . . .' (John 3.16). With this well-known text we should compare Matt. 5.43–48, with its conclusion: 'There must be no limit to your goodness, as your heavenly Father's goodness knows no bounds' (Matt. 5.48; see also the parable of the good Samaritan at Luke 10.26–38). The love spoken of here is not love between like-minded people or the love which is expressed only when it is likely to be reciprocated (Matt. 5.46a).

Second, there is the adaptability of love. Paul, in seeking to be 'all things to all men' (I Cor. 9.22) was the great apostolic practitioner of this. 'To the Jews,' he wrote, 'I became as a Jew . . . to those outside the Law as one outside the Law' (vv.20, 21a). Such crossing and re-crossing of community boundaries – in this case, Jew and Gentile – may explain his statement (II Cor. 11.24), 'Five times I received the thirty-nine strokes from the Jews'; that is, such punishment may have been the price he paid for readmission to the synagogue. As a Protestant to Protestants, as a Catholic to Catholics in Northern Ireland, provides a modern analogy. That is love's adaptability.

If love is the second aspect of the divine imprint on human life, hope is the third. Hope is the hardest of this Christian triad for us to grasp in our context, and there may be many reasons for this. Again, the biblical meaning has to be distinguished from contemporary usage. Christian hope is not the same as optimism, which derives from a person's temperament or circumstances. Nor is it 'hoping for the best', uncertain whether the best will materialize or not. By contrast, hope in the Bible seems to be born *in extremis* . Hope finds its clearest expression in the Bible when there is nothing to hope for and no one to hope in, except God and his promises. For Paul, Abraham provided a scriptural example of hope as well as of faith: 'When hope seemed hopeless, his faith was such that he became "father of many nations"' (Rom. 4.18).

This is why hope is frequently linked in the New Testament with suffering – suffering, that is, because a person is a disciple of Christ – and with endurance (e.g. Rom. 12.12). So hope is born when things look profoundly uncertain from a human point of view, and when they do so precisely because that is the apparent impasse to which a person's commitment to God has brought them. Even if they *feel* abandoned (Mark 15.34), 'the God of hope' creates life even out of death. So hope, in the Bible, unlike normal human hopes, has no visible support:

'When hope seemed hopeless his faith (i.e. Abraham's) was such that he became "father of many nations", in fulfilment of the promise, "so shall your descendents be"' (Rom. 4.18). Hope, by definition, is hope for something we do not yet see (Rom.8.25). Not surprisingly, the New Testament insists that such hope is the gift of the Holy Spirit (Rom. 5.5 and 15.13).

So, to summarize this section of the argument, the divine imprint on human life has as its fundamental pattern, faith, love and hope – all the work of the Holy Spirit. And if the divine Sonship of Jesus is taken seriously as the prototype of everyone else's, then it follows that this pattern too, like the contours of the Kingdom, and a cruciform existence, was imprinted on his life as well.

This final chapter has focussed on the question of God according to the New Testament, and I have suggested that the New Testament's answer is *God for us* . We have seen that, however dimly the mystery of God is perceived, the God of whom the New Testament speaks shares his life, his Kingdom, his righteousness, his love, his Spirit. He is the Father; all are potentially sons and daughters. There is one further example to be examined, and that is God's glory.

The glory of God, one might think, is, by definition, something which cannot be anyone else's. In the Old Testament this concept is closely related to the divine honour. The Hebrew *kabod* originally meant 'weight' – that which deserved recognition, or that which made a person impressive. It subsequently came to mean the divine radiance, as in Ex. 40.34–35: '. . . the glory of the Lord filled the tabernacle'. (Luke 2.9 is a New Testament example.)

It is John's Gospel which, more than any other New Testament writing, explores the meaning of the divine glory (*doxa*) in the light of Jesus Christ. There are three fundamental emphases to note. First, according to John's prologue, this glory was focussed in one person: 'So the Word became flesh; he made his home among us, and we saw his glory, such glory as befits the Father's only Son, full of grace and truth' (1.14). Here, the word 'glory' is defined or described, in a Greek translation of Old Testament language, as 'full of grace and truth'. As commentators point out, 'grace and truth' mean God's undeserved mercy and faithfulness to his own being.

The second chapter of the Gospel indicates how this divine glory impinges on human life. The story of Jesus turning water into wine at Cana-in-Galilee (2.1–11) ends with a broad hint from the writer that there is more to this miracle than first meets the eye: 'So Jesus performed at Cana-in-Galilee the first of the signs which revealed his glory and led his disciples to believe in him' (v.11, REB translation). In the light of the associations of wine with God or the gods in both the Jewish world (e.g. many OT prophecies portray wine in abundance as one of the blessings of God's future for his people), and in the wider Graeco-Roman world, this story is at least as much a parable as a miracle. Turning water into wine is a 'sign' pointing to eternal life, and it is precisely in the sharing of this gift that God's glory is revealed. But, as the exchange of Jesus with his mother suggests (vv.3–5), the revelation here at Cana is anticipatory.

That brings us to the second point. According to chapters 13 and 17 of this Gospel (13.31, 17.1), this glory was revealed in the hour when the Son of Man was 'lifted up'. This being 'lifted up', on the cross and in resurrection – John's special word embraced both – *is* the revelation of this undeserved mercy and faithfulness.

We noted in chapter 2 how the writer makes an important word-link between his introduction to the second half of the Gospel (13.1) and Jesus' final words on the cross (19.20). Jesus was now to show the full extent (*eis telos*) of his love for his own (13.1) and that, the writer indicates, came to pass in his death with the cry 'It is accomplished' (*tetelestai*) (19.30). So the cross in John is, paradoxically, Jesus' finest hour, the hour of his glory and, *at the same time*, because Father and Son are one, the revelation of God's glory, as this Gospel has defined that glory.

The third aspect to note is that the divine glory, like God's Kingdom and God's Spirit, is *shared*: 'The glory which you gave me I have given to them, that they may be one, as we are one' (17.22). So the revelation means that sharing the divine glory, given the meaning of this 'glory', is a task as well as a privilege. That glory is revealed in and, it would seem, only in, the love shown in and by the community of disciples.

'Eternal life is not so much an inheritance, as a mission.'[6] That is the significance of the imprint of the God for us.

A book about 'The Question of God' could be taken to mean that God is a problem to be investigated and solved. We are the agents, God the object of inquiry. The language of the New Testament suggests otherwise. In *Surprised by Joy* (note the passive verb), C.S. Lewis wrote of how he had thought that in his religious explorations he was playing patience, but discovered, in the end, that it was poker. He was not the only 'player', not only an enquirer; he was also being sought and addressed.

Such an experience resonates with New Testament language about God. It takes two to make a revelation, and if we have stressed the necessity of a recipient, we must note the New Testament also emphasizes the other dimension: '. . . no one knows the Son but the Father, and no one knows the Father but the Son, and those to whom the Son chooses to reveal him' (Matt. 11.27).

Human beings may seem to be the initiators, the agents, the ones who know, but in reality it is not so. The Bible does not attempt to reconcile what theologians have traditionally called 'predestination' with human responsibility. Human responsibility and the divine will inter-weave and interact throughout its pages. But it is vital to recognize that God does not reduce human beings to the status of puppets on a string. Human responsibility is enhanced, not overriden.

Now we see only puzzling reflections in a mirror, but one day we shall see face to face. Now I know in part, then I shall know, even as I am known (I Cor. 13.12).

Conclusion

I began by attempting to present the studies which are the core of this book in a wider context. In this brief conclusion I propose to end by trying, similarly, to relate these studies to wider issues. Three urgent problems, in particular, present themselves.

Ours is an age in which the Bible is a problem for many who call themselves Christians. What was called a generation ago 'The Strange Silence of the Bible in the Church'[1] remains largely true. Even if the problem is not always or often acknowledged, it is still no less of a problem. Those Christians who find the Bible quite *un*problematical merely reinforce the misgivings of those who do. The situation is both illustrated and made worse by the growing ignorance of the Bible, by the infrequency (it would seem), of serious Bible study, or of preaching which seriously attempts to explore and expound the meaning of the Bible for today.

It is possible that recent shifts in biblical scholarship may help. Scholars are no longer so preoccupied with historical questions such as the authorship and sources of our documents, and the history behind them – tasks which inevitably involve analysing and getting behind the texts, as far as possible. Instead, texts tend to be studied as narratives, as rhetoric, and, by some scholars, with attention to their final form and place in their canonical context. There is also a growing interest in the history of the interpretation of texts – a welcome recognition that this generation is not the first to grapple with some of the difficulties of these writings, and that there may be much to learn from the insights of earlier centuries. There is a danger, it has to be said, of lurching from one extreme to the other: in this case, from being too preoccupied with what really happened to thinking that what really happened doesn't matter at all. It *does* matter, but history is not the whole story.

The newer approaches may indirectly help Christian communities to re-appropriate (without, it is to be hoped, domesticating), the Bible for themselves. Whether that proves to be so or not, the scriptures must be read with faith, imagination, prayer and love, read privately and in groups, and preferably in groups whose leaders en-able, rather than dis-able the group.

A second problem, not unrelated to the first is the aridity and/or shallowness of much contemporary worship. Many Christians in this matter find themselves between a rock and a hard place: the choice between traditional worship (where 'traditional' need not mean 'boring', but often does), and worship which may be lively, but often lacks depth. This problem is often described in consumerist language (a worrying phenomenon in itself). We speak of 'catering for all tastes' and ' providing people with a choice in worship'. There is some truth in all this. Not all like the same music, nor should they be expected to do so. But where the sense of Christian family – or community, if that word is preferred – is strong, it ought to be possible to find a unity and diversity in worship and fellowship which meets people at a level far deeper than 'catering for different tastes'.

Thirdly, we have to reckon with the increasing marginal-ization or privatization of religion in our culture. This can be seen, for example, in our much more secular Sundays, in the diminishing place of religious broadcasting in TV schedules and, more generally, in the widespread assumption that religion is a spare-time activity and one's own private affair.

The reasons for these developments are many and complex. But it is vital, in such a situation, that Christians nourish a concrete sense of what God is doing in the world.[2] Without that, the temptation to withdraw into religious ghettoes will be all the stronger, and such ghettoes, even if they appear warm and cosy, will be increasingly barren and empty.

Thus far, I have identified three problems. Much more, of course, could be said of the crisis of contemporary Christianity in a period of bewildering change, fragmentation and uncertainty. But it is the background against which this book has been written, and I conclude with three specific proposals, however basic they may seem.

1. *The need to read the Bible*

This sounds simple and obvious. But in the kind of environment I have described in which most of us now live, and where most of us are too busy for our own good, this cannot be taken for granted. In any case, there is, I suspect, a further difficulty. The sheer volume of reading material (and, sometimes, its quality) available to us means that we easily lose the art of reflective reading. But skimming the Bible, whether for information or edification, is not perhaps the best way to read scripture. Reading the Bible is closely related to prayer.

Many modern daily Bible-reading schemes make that connection, but useful though such reading schemes may be, they tend to encourage the reading of the Bible in small chunks. Modern liturgical developments mean that we often *hear* the Bible in small chunks as well. Some will say that modern attention spans make it impossible to do otherwise. But it has to be asked whether, in so doing, we are making the most of the Bible.

David Ford, Regius Professor of Divinity at Cambridge University, has written challengingly on this subject. In a paper originally given to church leaders in the north of England, he suggests the application of what he calls 'practices of excess' to our use of the Bible:

> it is . . . worth allowing ourselves to become more intensively involved with some particular part of the Bible from time to time: read it slowly and repeatedly, meditate long on particular verses, themes, or images; study it alone and in groups, link it up with all the major doctrines of the Christian faith, range through the commentaries over the centuries and from different traditions (where relevant looking at Jewish authors), let it enter your prayer, your imagination, your conversation, and your sermons. In short, try to inhabit the text in every way possible.
>
> Without this sort of immersion, we cannot be gripped sufficiently by the Bible today, particularly in the culture we inhabit where the Bible is like a foreign language. We should not underestimate the erosion of Christian imagination and understanding that is taking place, even among faithful churchgoers, because of the flood of powerful ideas, images and stories that wash over us daily. In the face of such excesses, the least we need is a practice of excess that gives some chance of us being shaped even more comprehensively, imaginatively and intelligently by biblical ideas, images and stories'.[3]

2. *The need to relate the Old and New Testaments*

These days the Old Testament is neglected even more than the New. There are many reasons for this: some liturgical, some theological, some cultural.[4] For example, the greater prevalence of family, or 'all-age' worship, and of parish communion, means that those leading worship will omit the Old Testament lection, if it is difficult or obscure, or omit in favour of epistle and gospel if only two readings are required.

As for theological difficulties, the basic problem is well known. Either Christians see no problem in narratives in which (for example) God authorizes the massacre of the Amalekites, or we tend to dismiss the Old Testament as having a sub-Christian view of God. One view underestimates or ignores the difference between the Old and New Testaments, the other overestimates and distorts it.

The Hebrew scriptures have always been part of the Christians' Bible. Indeed, they were the church's Bible in the period before 'the New Testament' as such came into being (though Gentile Christians knew them in their Greek form – the so-called Septuagint). But the scriptures of Israel, though Christian scripture as well, do not have precisely the same status or function for Christians as they do for Jews. And that for two reasons. First, and most obviously, the church has, not just the Hebrew Bible, but a 'new testament', and, second, for the Christian, the heart of the scriptures is Christ himself. He is the 'canon within the canon' (where 'canon' means literally 'norm' or ' measuring rod'). If we apply this, for instance, to the Psalms, we are bound to say that the Christian cannot endorse all the prayers and aspirations of the psalmist, including the heartfelt prayers for the destruction of the wicked. But it is significant that the early church heard, as it were, the voice of Christ in the Psalms, particularly in the laments of the suffering righteous man: 'For Christ did not please himself; but as it is written, "The insults of those who insult you have fallen on me"' (Rom. 15.3, quoting Ps. 69.9; cf. John 19.24 and Heb. 10.7). It follows that the God to whom the psalmists cry again and again from the depths, and whom they praise, again and again, with their whole being, is the God and Father of our Lord Jesus Christ. So the church has always believed. So there is a solidarity in suffering and praise between Old and New Testaments, even whilst there are tensions and differences. Neither element must be overlooked or glossed over. To read the Old Testament – at length and in depth, in the way advocated by David Ford above – is the best way to get to grips both with its undoubted difficulties and the profundity of its theology.

3. The need for faithful living

In a sense nothing needs to be said about this. All Christians know it. Yet it may be useful to spell out its connection with the kind of Bible study I have tried to engage in here. Despite what is often said and thought, the church owes much to the work of biblical scholarship over the last few hundred years (since the Renaissance and Reformation). An enormous amount of work has been done to illuminate the origins, background, and not least, the many obscurities of the Bible. It is hardly too much to say that we are in a position to know more about the Bible than any generation before us, and so, in theory at least, we are better placed than previous generations to avoid some misunderstandings of the Bible and to make some sense of its more difficult passages. So far, so good, one might say. How ironical and tragic it would be, therefore, if the generation which could know more about the Bible than any before it were to read it the least, or to be the least faithful in heeding its testimony!

People can and do study the Bible without any faith commitment. That is their right and privilege, and people of faith may sometimes learn much from them. But I suspect that in a secular age increasingly few will study the Bible unless impelled by such a faith commitment, and one might wonder, anyway, whether there is much point in reading the Bible unless one is persuaded of the truth of the revelation to which it bears witness, or wishes to discover whether it is true. For the central subject matter of the Bible is God, and it is difficult to imagine a more important theme.

Notes

Introduction

1. M. J. Buckley SJ, *At the Origins of Modern Atheism*, Yale University Press 1987.
2. T. Kelly, *A Testament of Devotion*, Hodder & Stoughton, 2nd edn 1957, p.105.

1 Jesus and his God

1. G. Dalman, *The Words of Jesus*, T. & T. Clark 1902, p.196.
2. Ibid., p.194.
3. These criteria, much discussed by New Testament scholars, are attempts to distinguish original sayings of Jesus from (a) early church interpretation and (b) the additions (redactional work) of the evangelists themselves. The presence in the Gospel of the same sayings in different forms (notably the Lord's Prayer) suggests that such interpretations and additions have been made. Of course, Jesus may have said the same thing in different ways, but it has to be remembered that (a) Matthew and Luke almost certainly used Mark, and so some differences between them and Mark are likely to be their own work, and (b) some of the variations reflect the language and theology of each evangelist.

    The criterion of dissimilarity is the most radical of these criteria: where a saying clearly cannot be attributed to contemporary Judaism, or to the early church, it may be safely said to go back to Jesus himself (e.g. Matt. 8.22/Luke 9.60). This has a limited usefulness but, as has often been pointed out, this criterion ignores the common ground between Jesus and both Judaism and the early church. (Why can't Jesus have said something which could equally well have been said by either?)

4. See especially Bruce D. Chilton, *God in Strength*, JSOT Sheffield 1987. It is probable that in his native Aramaic, Jesus would have referred either to 'the Kingdom', or to 'the Kingdom of Heaven'.

5. G. F. Moore, *Judaism*, Cambridge University Press 1927, Vol.2, p.204.

6. T.W. Manson, *The Teaching of Jesus*, Cambridge University Press 1951, p.101.

7. Ibid., pp.104–5

8. Dalman, op.cit., p.283.

9. In a discussion of the teaching of Jesus in *Studying the Synoptic Gospels*, SCM Press 1989, E. P. Sanders and M. Davies examine possible parallels in OT and Jewish teaching to these particular commands of Jesus. They tend to under-estimate the originality of the first command, 'Love your Enemies', and to argue for the uniqueness of the second, 'Pray for your persecutors'. More important, Sanders and Davies overlook the fact that the texts referred to here, e.g. Ex. 23.4, 5, apply to an all-Israelite context. 'The enemy' envisaged in Exodus would not be a Gentile. It might be argued that that possibility is not evident in Matthew either. But the earlier, almost certain reference to the Roman military, 'If anyone compels you to go with him one mile, go with him two' (v.41) implies that the subsequent commands embrace Jew and Gentile alike.

10. W. F. Lofthouse, *The Father and the Son*, SCM Press 1934, p.76.

11. Ibid., p.75

12. J. Jeremias, *New Testament Theology*, SCM Press 1971, pp.9–14.

13. S. Schechter, *Studies in Judaism*, quoting Ben Azzai, Meridian 1957, pp.107–8.

14. That is, such a saying may have been difficult for the early church, which would therefore have been unlikely to have created such a saying. The story of Jesus' baptism, as told by Matthew and Luke, is a good example of an 'embarrassing' detail which these two writers at least may have found difficult.

15. The parallel with the prayer of Stephen (Acts 7.59) indicates that Luke 23.34 is original, and that the MSS variants here (with several important MSS omitting it) should be attributed to the ugly antisemitism which surfaced only too quickly in subsequent centuries.

2 *The Crucified God*

1. Most of these writings cannot be dated with any precision, but the Wisdom of Solomon may well be the product of the first century AD. Alexandria has been suggested as a possible place of origin. I Enoch is a composite work, and may derive from the first centuries BC and AD. (The part known as the Parables or Similitudes of Enoch is the hardest of all to date, but may be one of the later sections.) The apocalypses IV Ezra and II Baruch are a response to the destruction of Jerusalem in AD 70, and so belong to the late first century AD or even, in the case of II Baruch, to the early second century. The Psalms of Solomon are probably earlier, reflecting awareness of events in the first century BC. Philo of Alexandria took part in a Jewish delegation to Rome in AD 39 or 40. The Dead Sea Scrolls, the literature of the Qumran Community, probably belong to the first two centuries BC.

2. E. P. Sanders, *Paul and Palestinian Judaism*, SCM Press 1977.

3. The translation is that of Geza Vermes.

4. Josephus, *Antiquities* 4.201, and *Apologia* 2.166.

5. If a comma is meant to follow the reference to Christ ('the Messiah'), then Christ is being addressed as God ('. . . God blessed forever'). If, however, a full stop is intended, then he is not.

6. We should note that many scholars think Colossians was written by a disciple of Paul. This does not affect its authority, but it clearly affects what we regard as Paul's own theology. This is especially important for what we have called the 'pre-existence' of Christ, since Col. 1.15–20 (a kind of Wisdom hymn about Christ) is the most extended language of this kind in the New Testament epistles (though see also Heb. 1.1–4).

7. II Cor. 5.19 ('For God was in Christ . . .') *sounds* like incarnational language and, indeed, may be, but there are a number of unusual features about the Greek which make it less than certain.

8. John T. Fitzgerald, *Cracks in an Earthen Vessel*, Scholars Press, Atlanta 1988.

9. In *Theology and Ethics in Paul and His Interpreters*. Essays in Honour of Victor Paul Furnish ed E. H. Lovering Jr. and J. L. Sumney, Abingdon Press, Nashville 1966, pp.83–99.

10. W. F. Lofthouse, *The Father and the Son*, SCM Press 1934, pp. 79–80.
11. The Targums, Aramaic translations/paraphrases of the Hebrew scriptures, are notoriously difficult to date, but probably reflect some traditions contemporary with Jesus and Paul. The Book of Jubilees is thought to originate in the second century BC.
12. Paul's language here becomes almost impossible to translate: *hypereperisseusen he charis*: grace 'super-abounded'.

3 When the Image Fades

1. F. Watson, *Text, Church, and World*, T. & T. Clark 1995.
2. 'Faith in Gods and in God' from *Radical Monotheism and Western Culture* by H. Richard Niebuhr, Harper & Row 1960; reprinted in *The Theologian at Work* ed A. Roy Eckardt, SCM Press 1968, pp.53–54.
3. A. Heschel, *The Prophets*, Harper & Row 1962, p.282
4. Ibid., p.292.
5. J. Ziesler, *Paul's Letter to the Romans*, SCM Press 1989, p.75.
6. C. E. B. Cranfield, *Romans*, Vol. 1 (ICC), T. & T. Clark 1975, p.118.
7. J. A. T. Robinson, *Wrestling With Romans*, SCM Press 1979, p.20
8. P. Fiddes, *The Creative Suffering of God*, Clarendon Press 1992, p.24.
9. Heschel, op. cit., pp.299–305.
10. Robinson, op. cit. p.20.
11. S. E. Ballentine, *The Hiddenness of God*, Oxford University Press 1983.
12. R. Bultmann, *The Gospel According to John*, Blackwell 1971, p.154.
13. A. Cadoux, *The Theology of Jesus*, Nicholson & Watson 1940, p.82.
14. L. T. Johnson, *Sharing Possessions*, SCM Press 1981, p.46.
15. W. Pannenberg, *Christian Spirituality and Sacramental Community*, Darton, Longman and Todd 1982, pp.90–91.
16. Ibid., p.92

4 *The Question of God*

1. S. Moore, *The Fire and the Rose are One*, Darton, Longman and Todd 1980, p.35.
2. Whatever originally happened in these miracles (the feeding miracles, Jesus stilling the storm, and walking on the water), the role of the disciples in these narratives makes them, in effect, *church*-miracles.
3. In the Old Testament, 'creating' and 'calling' are closely associated activities of God.
4. Philo's works are to be found in the Loeb Classical Library (12 vols, Heineman 1929–53), available in most academic theological libraries.
5. C. S. Lewis' distinctions between four different Greek words in his popular book *The Four Loves* are misleading. The meanings of the words vary and overlap with one another.
6. A. T. Cadoux, *The Theology of Jesus*, Nicholson & Watson 1940, p.19.

Conclusion

1. The title of a book by James D. Smart, published by SCM Press in 1970.
2. See W. Brueggemann's *Hopeful Imagination. Prophetic Voices in Exile*, SCM Press 1986, p.16.
3. David D. Ford, 'Coping with being Overwhelmed', published by The Bible Society in *Transmission*, Autumn 1997.
4. On this see especially Stephen Barton's *Invitation to the Bible*, SPCK 1997, ch. 3, 'Two Testaments, One Bible'.